OZARK IKE
MEMORIES OF FENCE BUSTER
Gus Zernial

by Gus Zernial

with Ronnie Joyner & Bill Bozman

Published by Pepperpot Productions, Inc.
P.O. Box 1016
Dunkirk, MD 20754

Written and designed by Ronnie Joyner and Bill Bozman.

Table of Contents

Bobby Shantz and I are hamming it up a bit before a game.

Foreword

by: Bobby Shantz

I was truly honored when Gus asked me to write the Foreword for his book. I wanted to be short and sweet with my thoughts, and in trying decide what to say, my initial thought of Gus was simple — I had a heck of a time getting him out when he played for the White Sox. As a matter of fact, I was probably the happiest guy on our club when I learned we had acquired Gus, along with Dave Philley. It was a three-way deal that involved the A's, White Sox and Indians. I really hated to pitch against him as he looked like a angry giant at the plate. He was 6'-4" tall, and his bat always seemed so long to me. He just flat-out looked so mean up at the plate — and he was a heck of a hitter!

When he and Dave joined our club I found out the real truth about Gus. He wasn't mean at all. Turns out, he was one of the nicest guys I would ever know. I was certainly glad he was on our side though. For me, that particular trade really paid dividends quickly. In 1952, I won 24 games and the American League MVP award — I think the big bat of Gus Zernial may have accounted for a dozen of my wins that season. Gus hit 42 home runs that year, and it seemed that he hit half of them, when I was on the mound. He had such a beautiful swing, and he didn't hit cheap homers either — his four baggers went a long way. Gus had played for our manager, Jimmie Dykes, earlier in Chicago and he really liked Gus, both as a hitter and a fine person. I imagine those were key reasons the trade was made.

I remember Gus as a really easy going guy and a good family man. I don't think there was a guy on our team that didn't like him. As I said before, I know one thing for sure — I certainly was happy to have him as a teammate.

What is so nice these days is seeing my old friends at baseball gatherings. We have the Philadelphia Athletics Historical Society, which gets many of the former ballplayers together during the year. The likes of Joe DeMaestri, Bill Renna, Joe Astroth, Eddie Joost, Spook Jacobs, and many others, are all invited back each year to socialize and have a little "bull" session, as well as a nice breakfast. Anyway, Gus always gives a short speech at the breakfast telling everyone how nice he thinks it is to be remembered, and he's certainly right. We players really appreciate that after all the years. And, after all these years, I consider Gus Zernial one of my best friends!

An Introduction
Baseball and Gus Zernial

The purpose of writing this book is recounting my life experiences, both in and away from baseball. My hope is that it will reach both younger and older baseball fans. There are so many stories that come from this great game, I can't even begin to scratch the surface. Things like what the game meant to me; what mark did I leave on the game; and what I got out of the game.

I was lucky enough to play with and against many Hall of Fame ball players. I played for many managers, general managers and team owners. The game of baseball is truly a kid's game. It's played professionally, by men with great skill and ability. Some gave 110%, and many of those players became stars. Some gave much less and became the ones that just fill out the lineup card. Meeting people in the game — the players, managers and administration folks — became my baseball education. I spent 11 years getting my high school diploma. I then tacked on another 11 years getting my education in attitude, competitive skill and the business of baseball. When I left baseball in 1960, I often said, "In the business world, baseball qualified me for absolutely nothing." In retrospect, that simply was not so. Later, I realized, that baseball opened many doors for me in that world. Doors were opened for me to be the sports director of a radio and television station. It led me to a career in marketing and public relations, and so many others things in my business life. Today, I am getting so much from baseball. It really is true — you get out of the game just as much as you put in.

It also took me a few years to realize what the fans meant to the game. Whether it was Chicago, Philadelphia, Kansas City or Detroit, the fans always had something to give to the players. This also goes for the cities we visited too. I always wanted to play well in every town, because it may have been the first time a fan in that city had ever seen me play. Today, I often get mail from fans that say they saw me play, which is great to hear. I even get letters from youngsters that say they didn't see me play, but their father or grandfather did. I always tried to be the best I could be everyday for that reason. A Hall of Fame player once said, "Give your best everyday — it may the first or last time a fan may get to see you play." I tried to play every game that way.

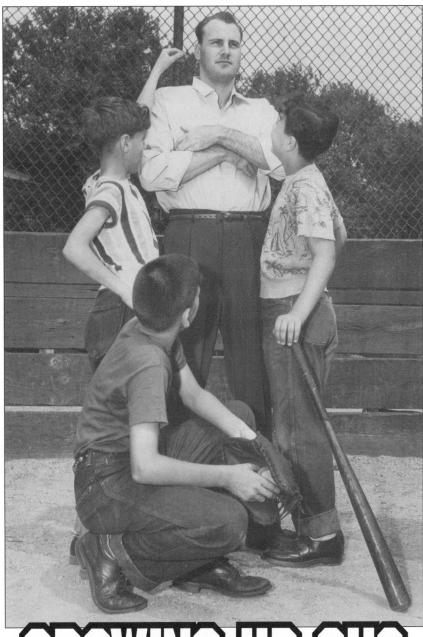

GROWING UP GUS

A Kid's Life

Growing up in Beaumont

Like many young men, wanting to become an athlete, I came from a poor but loving family in Beaumont, Texas. Gustavious Emile Zernial and Emma Caroline had 10 children in all. I was the youngest of those kids but grew up with just six brothers and sisters. Before I was born, two of my sisters had died, the result of childhood diseases and one of my brothers had been killed in a hunting accident. At the writing of this book, three brothers and three sisters, as well as Mom and Dad, have gone to meet the Lord.

During my childhood, it was my Mom who taught me the most about life. She educated me in the ways of being a gentleman and always emphasized having character. Dad passed away when I was 15-years old — Mom was 60 at the time. She raised me with the help of my brothers and sisters.

Reflecting on my childhood always makes me want to begin at the age of 7 years old. Now everyone knows that moms have always done a lot for their children, but my Mom was extra special because of my health circumstances. As a young boy of 7 years, I had just started school and I contracted a pneumonia which affected my heart. Doctors diagnosed me with an enlarged heart. I was in bed for 9 months. Though I was not feeling sick I had to be kept very quiet.

Before the pneumonia I was always looking for a group of kids to play baseball with. An empty lot or a park playground to play a game, or maybe just the side of a barn to toss a ball towards and catch it. We had tough winters in my home town of Beaumont, so baseball was truly a summer game. All that was gone for a long while for me, because of my heart condition. Both of my parents did so much for me during this time. I probably weighed 80 pounds, yet Mom would carry me from room to room. My Dad, a very hard working carpenter, would stop at the ice cream store to buy me a carton everyday. He had to walk about four blocks to get it and by the time he arrived home it would be a milk shake — but it was always good just the same.

Amazingly, being stricken ill when I was 7-years old, I wasn't allowed outside until I was 9! What Mom and Dad had to do with me was amazing. The first day out, all I wanted to do was chase the chickens all over the place.

14

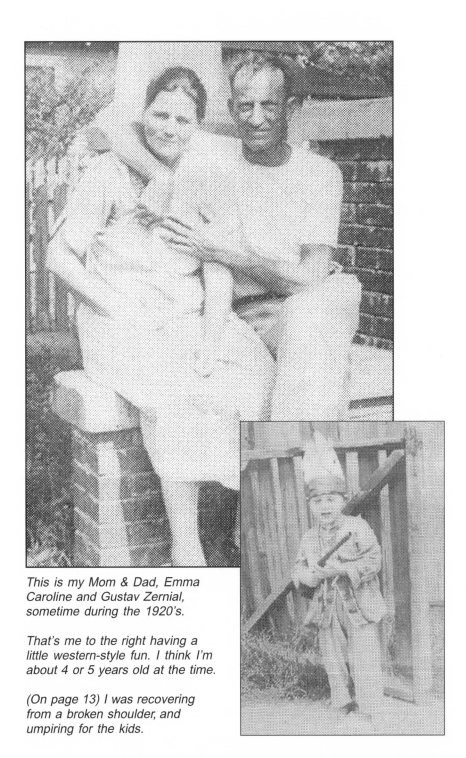

This is my Mom & Dad, Emma Caroline and Gustav Zernial, sometime during the 1920's.

That's me to the right having a little western-style fun. I think I'm about 4 or 5 years old at the time.

(On page 13) I was recovering from a broken shoulder, and umpiring for the kids.

Mom and Dad always raised chickens and would grow a healthy garden to fill our dinner table. While I was very spoiled, Mom disciplined me quite often. After all of that time cooped up (like a chicken), I guess I was bound to go a little crazy once I had a taste of freedom again.

This little incident happened soon after I was free to go outside. Mom had washed and ironed all day and upon finishing went to visit a neighbor. I guess in hindsight, unfortunately for me I was not invited. Well, I proceeded to mess up all the wash and ironed clothes. You know how fun that can be as a bored child. When Mom returned home she didn't raise her voice or even get mad. She just said, "Son, get me a switch off the peach tree out back so I can spank you." Well, to further aggravate an already bad situation, I went out and broke off half of the tree — it seemed like the clever thing to do at the time. Leave it to Mom because she found about 50 switches on that half of a tree, and she wore my butt and legs out with all 50 of them. Did I ever learn my lesson! You can bet I never had to be switched again. She continued to do great things for me after that, just as before. I have so much respect for both of my parents.

Working my way back into the a regular kid's life really concerned my Mom at this time. I was 9-years old in June, and school was to start in September. The only schooling I knew was from Mom and our home schooling sessions. Can you imagine a 9-year old sitting in the first grade with 6 and 7 year old children? Leave it all to Mom though — she sold the principal and teachers on a great game plan. They kept me in the first grade for a few weeks and I did all right. I was then promoted to the second grade at mid-term, then moved on to the third grade soon after and was able to handle it all. Luckily, I had caught up with my class. In reality, I only spent 3 years in elementary school and graduated to the sixth grade. Smart kid, huh?

I grew up with the Woosley family. My oldest sister, Henrietta, married a gentleman by the name of Earl Woosley. They had three children, Betty Lee, Earl (or Pete as he was called) and David. Pete and Betty were like a brother and sister to me. As I mentioned earlier, my Dad passed away when I was 15-years old so I became like a son to Earl and Henrietta. I still had my brothers and sisters around, of course, to help take care of Mom and I. My entire family became very devoted baseball fans of yours truly. We truly had a family of love.

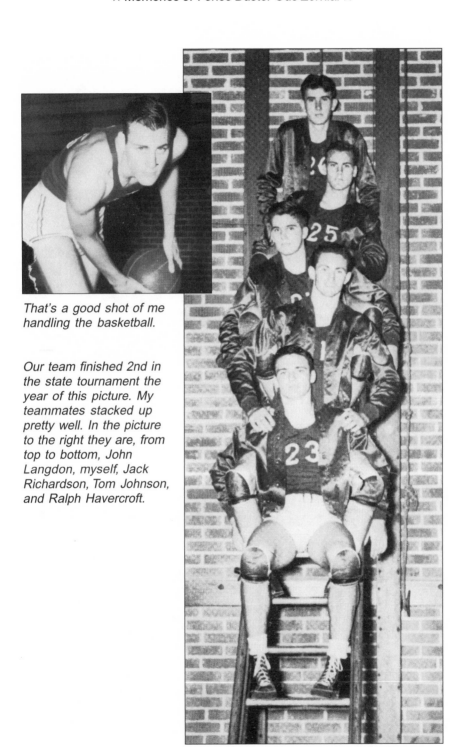

That's a good shot of me handling the basketball.

Our team finished 2nd in the state tournament the year of this picture. My teammates stacked up pretty well. In the picture to the right they are, from top to bottom, John Langdon, myself, Jack Richardson, Tom Johnson, and Ralph Havercroft.

Up top I have just scored a
basket, laying the ball.

To the right is a shot of me
as we run through a few
practice drills. I really enjoyed
the game of basketball.

As I grew older, going into junior high and high school, I participated in all sports. I played football, basketball, track, and, of course, baseball. I remember so well many of my friends and teammates on all those teams. In basketball it was Ken Currey, Ralph Havercroft, Tom Johnson, Jack Richardson and John Langdon who all became successful in life. In baseball, I played on the same team with Grady Hatton, who played in the major leagues for over 10 seasons. I can't forget my high school coaches, Raymond Alford (a great athlete at Baylor University), Buddy Savage and Moody Pickett. And how could I talk about high school and not mention a girlfriend or two, like Betty DeMary and Barbara Collier. Incidentally, I was a 3-year letterman in basketball and captain my senior year, and 3-year letterman in baseball. I received scholarships to Baylor and Oklahoma.

As a young man growing up, I followed professional baseball very closely. My hometown of Beaumont, Texas, was home to the farm team of the Detroit Tigers of the American League. I was about 15 years old when the likes of Hank Greenberg, Rudy York, Birdie Tebbets, Virgil Trucks, Hal Newhouser, Benny McCoy, Pat Mullin, Barney McCosky and many more like them were in town playing ball. Not only did I get to see these guys play, but later, when I made it to the major leagues, I had the good fortune to play with or against them. As all kids who follow ball clubs and go to the park see them play, I have a few knothole gang stories I'll spill later in the book.

Remember, I mentioned my two girlfriends in my senior year, Barbara and Betty. Betty was a senior, and Barbara a freshman. I didn't know they knew each other and I liked them both during my senior year. So one day I got this really clever idea. I gave Barbara my freshman lettermen jacket to wear and handed my senior jacket over to Betty. Some of you can identify with and see where this story is going. There was a lunch gathering on the lawn on campus and you guessed it — both were having lunch together. Needless to say, I got both jackets back and lost two friends. You really learn both in and out of the classroom in high school and sometimes it's the hard way.

My senior year was 1941, and during that summer I got one of my many great thrills in the game of baseball. I went to a rookie tryout held by the St. Louis Cardinals, held under the guidance of none other than Baseball Hall of Fame member Branch Rickey. I was one of the lucky 3 players that got a professional baseball assignment — and let me tell you there were a lot of kids there for the 3-day tryout. I was 17 at the time. This was in May of 1941 and I wouldn't be 18 until June of that same year. They wanted me to go home and talk with my family and report to a rookie league in Hamilton, Ontario, in Canada. I had never been very far from home in Beaumont and you can imagine what went through my mind. I went home and told Mom what they wanted me to do and I asked her where Hamilton, Ontario, was. Now I had studied geography in school, but I sure didn't know where Hamilton was. Mom and I decided not to report for the rest of that summer. Our decision not to report made us wonder where would they send me in 1942?

Meet My Dad
A lasting impression on me

Before I get into the beginning of my professional baseball career, I want to tell you a little bit about my Dad. While writing this book, I thought of him quite often. I didn't get to bond with my Dad like having him come and watch me play sports in school. Though, now, I think a great deal about the life we did share together. The most vivid memories I have of my Dad are when I was about 7-years old. I started school, and suddenly was stricken with a pneumonia which kept me in bed at home for over 18 months. It was really my Mom that took care of me at home — Dad had to work. When he returned from work, I would always be at the window waiting for him as he would bring me an ice cream treat.

My Dad was born in 1874, making him a handsome 26-year old at the turn of the century in 1900 — my Mom would have been 21. Looking back, I really like the relationship my folks had — after all, they were to have 10 children in all. I was born on June 27, 1923, and that would make my Dad 49-years old at the time of my birth. I would be child number 10. My sisters and brothers all said I was a mistake — aren't siblings great?

My Dad was a pool hall jockey — he really liked to play pool. But pool took a back seat to playing dominoes, and betting on big league baseball games. You could bet $1.00, and pick the score or winners in five games. If you won three of the five picked, you would get $3.00 back. If you got all five you would win $10.00. I doubt he always came out on top, but I sure remember him winning a good percentage of time.

He drove a Model T Ford automobile, possibly the most complicated of any car to drive. He couldn't drive a regular shift car. The story goes that he could drive an open top Model T, and roll a Bull Durham cigarette at the same time. If you are not too impressed, keep this in mind — the car would travel at a speed of 20 mph and the tobacco was of the powder type. Henry Ford invented the Model T in the early 1900's. By 1930, the Great Depression had become a major fact of life for most families. Though I was only 10-years old in the early 1930's, I remember that time well, and just how difficult it was. My Dad was a carpenter, and he built many houses in Beaumont, Texas where I was born.

At an early age, maybe 12 or so, I would go with him on certain jobs. I was amazed then, and even now, at some of the things he could do in building. I recall being with him as he put a new roof on a two-story house. As I recall, the shingles came in bundles, and there were so many bundles that made up a square. Now, he didn't measure a thing mind you. We walked around the house for well over an hour, and finally he told me that we would need so many squares (and he stated the amount, which I don't remember) to complete this job and have a few bundles remaining to complete another one we had to do. Well, it took us about 3 weeks to complete that job, and wouldn't you know it — we had enough bundles left to do the other job. That was an incredible feat to me.

On another occasion, he was to build a barn as they were called at the time. Now, of course, the building you park your car in is called a garage. I was with him the first day. All he did was figure the amount of lumber he would need, and placed an order for it. The next day the lumber was promptly delivered. He then measured and marked numerous lines, and told me to saw on those lines. I did this for about 2 days straight, and stacked the cut pieces in certain rows as I was instructed. Upon completion of the cutting, he started calling for a certain length piece, and he would fit it into the proper position. This seemed like no minor task, and was simply amazing to me. I'll tell you to this day that he was the best carpenter in the world. That was the bonding time with my Dad — sort of on the job training if you will.

About this time, I started spending a lot of my time on the baseball fields, wherever I could find them. My Dad was getting older, and much slower too — walking didn't come nearly as easy as it had just a few years earlier. I recognized this, and many times would leave the field when I would see my Dad walking home. He would stop and rest, and I would escort him home. Many times, I would not head back to the field to play, but just hang around the house. He suffered with emphysema, a lung disease. Not very much was known about it in those days. It really bothered me to see my Dad suffer so much.

On Christmas Eve of 1938, at 10:00 PM, my Dad passed away. They say people have a sixth sense, and know when their time is up. I believe that is completely true. On that evening when we opened our Christmas gifts, he opened a gift from someone in the family. At the time, I was sitting right next to him. The gift was three pairs of socks, and he said to me, "You take these two pair, I won't need them." At 10:00 PM, he went to be with the Lord. Gustavious Emile, my Dad, never got to see me play any organized sport. I know, though, that he would have been proud of me. Fortunately, my Mother would see me play in the big show.

The photo on the opposite page shows me with Babe Ruth and my teammate, Frank Kelleher before a game at Gilmore Field in Hollywood, California. This photo was taken in 1948, not long before Babe passed away. Our public relations director asked if Babe would pose with us and he graciously did.

PAID TO PLAY

I'm a Professional

My first taste of baseball at the next level

Remember that question we had back in 1942? Well, the answer would arrive soon enough. Management of the Cardinals said they would like me to report to Albany, Georgia. Being southern folk, we knew where Albany was, and my new assignment was just fine with us. The funny thing about reporting for spring camp in Albany was being an old country boy, my attire was a pair of bib coveralls and some clodhopper shoes — now that's real country. I wasn't embarrassed though — I was there to play baseball and getting paid to do so! The start for me and many of the other players that would make it to the big leagues was much different than that of the players starting in the '60s and '70s. In the '30s and '40s, cars and clothing simply were not the biggest priority. We were typically hoping to earn enough for us to live on and send back a few dollars for the family — oh, how the times have changed!

When spring arrived in 1942, the world had changed quite a bit. The United States had been attacked in 1941 at Pearl Harbor and the country was at war. The European continent had been at war since 1939 when an evil ruler by the name of Adolf Hitler, the leader of Nazi Germany, was trying to conquer the world. We were attacked by Japan, so World War II was on. It was December 7, 1941, when the Japanese tore up Pearl Harbor. I was 18 in June of that same year and not eligible for the draft, so I reported to the St. Louis Cardinals minor league camp in Albany. I must tell you that at this time I was given a signing bonus. I got a one-way bus ticket to Albany, made the club and was playing centerfield.

World War II took its toll on minor league baseball. Many minor leagues had broken up due to the many players enlisting or being drafted. The Cards owned so many players that they had teams in most minor leagues. Whomever the Cards had that were not taken by the service were sent to Albany about a month into the season. I was hitting over .300 and playing a pretty good centerfield, but when others joined the team they had to cut the roster to 15 players. Joe Cusick, our manager, called me in and said he had to release me to keep a left-handed hitting outfielder. The main reason they wanted the left-hander was because Sportsman's Park in St. Louis was a left-handers paradise.

It was 310 feet down the right field line. Remember, the Cards had left-handed hitters and future Hall of Famers like John Mize, Stan Musial and Enos Slaughter. The manager wanted to find me another spot, but I declined and chose to head home. Fortunately, about two weeks later the Waycross team of the same Georgia-Florida League called and asked if I wanted to continue my career with them. I accepted and reported to Waycross. I finished the season playing in leftfield and hitting a respectable .289.

Other than playing ball, I found that not too much goes on in the lower minors. I played a lot of pool and tried to find a young lady to take to a movie — if you could find a movie house! And eating was always on the light side. We didn't get much meal money and our salary was only $65 a month. If you were a good talker you might get $75, but that was unusual. Nonetheless, it was the brightest light in my world.

Looking back, one of the more interesting things about my first year was the traveling and baseball tutoring. Let's take baseball first. You learned many of your baseball skills on your own. Things like what base to throw to on certain base hits or where the cutoff man may be located. And it seemed at that time that many of the other players didn't know where they should be, as there was no coach to tell him. It was not like today with multitude of coaches that all clubs have. Baseball in the minors in 1942 — you pretty much taught yourself. Having said all that, at 17 years of age I had put together a pretty good year. I was 6'-2" and weighed 180 pounds. Can you believe I was the lead-off man — I could run. We had a few 3-year minor league veterans on that ballclub and I watched and learned a lot from those guys.

The season ended in the middle of September and I was heading for home. I knew very well what was coming. Uncle Sam was not going to draft me for the Army, so on October 19, 1942, my nephew, Billy Zernial, and I joined the U.S. Navy. We joined in Beaumont, Texas, and were sent to boot camp in San Diego, California.

Navy Time

A speed bump in my baseball career

In 1942, with World War II in full swing, I began my time serving my country in the Navy. This effected people from all walks of life, including professional athletes. We looked at it simply as a war that had to be won — and that's what we did. Many big league baseball players, as well as minor, left to serve their country. I was a proud Navy Gob that served my time in the Pacific. We battled the Japanese subs, Q-boats, and those paper kites called Zeros. From 1942 through 1945, I had the same type of experiences so many did. I feel blessed to be one of the fortunate ones that returned.

During this time, I had a few baseball and boxing experiences that I still remember well. The first one happened upon the completion of a trip around the world. That journey took us to China, Burma and India. We landed on Treasure Island, a Navy base in San Francisco, during the summer of 1944. I played in some games with the 12th Navy District. One of the names related to those games I still remember well is Harry Chronert. He is still a friend today and, by the way, we won the district championship.

The boxing story is one that I will never forget. I was working out in the gym, doing a little shadow boxing. A gym rat approached me, and asked if I would go a couple of two-minute rounds with his buddy. Well, I weighed about 180 pounds and I quickly sized this other guy up — I guessed he was about 220 pounds. During the first round I held my own pretty well — I felt faster than he was. I was feeling pretty good about myself at the round's completion. The second round was a different story, though. At the start of the round, he caught me with a left hook and I felt like my nose had been plastered all over the gym. It was at that point that I figured he didn't want to spar, he wanted to knock my brains out! I left the ring trying to save some of my blood and asking, "Who the hell was that guy!" I was told he was the 12th District Navy heavyweight champ — that was the end of my boxing career.

For the trip around the world, I was aboard the *U.S.S. Vancouver*. It was a merchant ship and I was a radioman 3rd class. In addition, I manned a gun if we encountered any trouble. We left the dock in San Francisco with an aircraft cargo (I was told it was P-40's.) Our first stop was to be in Calcutta in

India — but our first encounter with the Japanese fleet was in the Indian Ocean, well before we arrived at our destination. The Japanese had a ship they called a Q-boat. This type of vessel was spotted in the early dawn, and general quarters was sounded. That meant everybody on deck and ready for battle. This Q-boat was very fast and maneuverable — it circled us all day. We knew, speed-wise, we were beaten, but the ship stayed on the horizon all day. We kept general quarters all night, and the next morning the ship was gone. At that point we were about 3 days out from Calcutta. We encountered no further problems, docked to drop our cargo, and met with Navy officials to discuss what had happened to us during our voyage. As I understood, the ship we had encountered was rigged to look like a merchant ship, but had the ability to drop its sides to reveal high-powered guns, able to sink any merchant ship like ours. The reason we were not attacked was the cargo we were carrying was in large boxes, stacked on top of one and other, then painted gray, the same color as the ship. The Japanese thought we were a counter Q-boat, a decoy if you will, the same as they were. They figured we were looking to attack their ship. That's what I call being saved by the cargo!

We spent 17 days in Calcutta and were bombed each day. Amazingly, our ship was never hit. There were 5 docks in the area, as it was a major supply line for both American and British ships. Many ships were hit and sunk during that time. Luck was definitely on our side during this time. After the 17 days, we left Calcutta for Durban in South Africa. I don't recall what cargo we were carrying at that time. Durban was a beautiful city and we spent 17 days there, as well. In Durban, I saw some of the biggest rickshaw runners I can remember — our football scouts would have had more recruits than they could ever imagine had they been there. The two things I remember most about the city were how clean it was, and how many pretty women were there — that's a nice combination!

Our next stop was Rio in Brazil — now there's a real playground. These places like Durban and Rio were well out of the war zone, and not bad places to be. That part if the trip was more like a pleasure cruise to me, with the exception of Calcutta. After 2 weeks in Rio we headed out, and into more trouble. We had orders to join 30 other ships in a convoy toward the east coast of Brazil and the United States. A Navy destroyer and two small escort vessels accompanied us back to New York. Off the coast of Virginia our convoy was attacked by a German submarine. The U-boat was defeated as the destroyer hit the sub with depth charges as she tried to dive. I was one happy sailor when we landed safely in New York.

I received a 15 day pass and traveled to see the family in Texas, then headed back to San Francisco, and Treasure Island, my home port. When I reached Treasure Island around February of 1944 I learned that my nephew, Billy Zernial, had been killed in the Pacific. Billy and I had joined the Navy together. My family calling the Navy, combined with normal military procedures, caused me to be held on base for a number of months after that. About the beginning of March of the same year I found out about 12th District Navy baseball team.

The 12th District Navy baseball team consisted of players that were all Petty Officers of a special branch of the Navy called Specialist-A. By this time I had gotten over much of the shock of my nephew's death, and was interested in playing for that Navy team, if I was able to get permission. My duty since ashore was to write a text on radio and flag signals while at sea. That was a 2 to 3 hour class, each day of the week. In the meantime, the Navy team was trying to get me permission to play with them. Unfortunately, this was not a simple task as the warrant officer simply would not grant me permission. The commander of Treasure Island, however, was an officer by the name of Flaherty. He turned out to be a true difference-maker for me and gave me the go-ahead to play. This really made me happy — I wish I could say the same for my warrant officer. Let me tell you — he was none too pleased at being over-ruled, and he let me know it. Nonetheless, my duties now were to play ball for the base and write my signal text. I completed my text in about 6 weeks, turned it in as required, and continued to play ball for the Naval base. We didn't play every day, but we had about 25 games, and we won the 12th Naval District title. During that time, my warrant officer would ask me every day, when the last game would be played. I really didn't know, so I couldn't tell him. He would tell me that I had better have my sea bag packed, because the day after it was over, I would be shipping out.

The season ended the last week of August. Commander Flaherty had a big celebration for us because we won the district championship. He gave each of us leave for 17 days. When I got back to my barracks, who do you think was waiting for me — you guessed it, my warrant officer. I never saw a

Up top I'm home on leave from the Navy during my time in the Pacific in World War II.

To the right is a shot of me just before leaving for Navy duty.

guy so ready, and happy to do his job. His job, of course, was to send me out to sea. We met in his office, and I told him that I could not report for sea duty right away because Commander Flaherty had granted me leave of 17 days. Well, as you can imagine, my warrant officer was fit to be tied. He had now been overruled twice. The funny thing is, I don't think he even knew the commander. I found out later, when we played a game on the base, that he had come out to see the team play. Turns out that he was actually a pretty nice guy. I took my leave, and upon my return to Treasure Island, was on a ship a mere 3 days later — sometimes the government does work quickly. Seems my name was at the top of the list for sea duty — on the third day back, I was packed, and on a ship bound for Portland, Oregon.

I was on base in Portland for a few weeks before I was assigned to another ship. I had only been on the ship for a couple days when I discovered that 3 civilians were on board to man the radio — my Navy training was in radio operation, and they didn't seem to need much help there. It was about this time that I made a second major discovery — we were stopping in San Francisco, and I was being sent to Treasure Island for a new assignment. Things sure weren't looking up for me now. This new turn of events meant I would be meeting my good friend, the warrant officer, all too soon for me. The ship was scheduled to leave the dock in Portland at 9:00 PM. I had about 6 hours of thinking time to make up my mind, which was more than enough — I decided to jump ship.

I asked one of my Navy mates if he could get my papers sent back by pilot boat, and return them to base. About 8:00 PM I went over the side, sea bag and all. Fortunately, I was friendly with all the officers on the Portland base. The next day I reported to base, as I didn't want to be AWOL (Absent Without Official Leave.) And, if jumping ship wasn't enough — every Saturday was inspection day in the Navy, and wouldn't you know the day I reported was Saturday.

Most of the people on base were aware of my act. I was instructed to sit in an office, and wait for a call from the commander's office, located in downtown Portland. About 10:00 AM I got the call. I dressed in my best Navy Togs, looking as clean and bright as I could, and headed downtown to meet the commander. When I reported, I remember him looking right at me, and saying, "Gus Zernial, have a seat." I must say, I was a little nervous about our

This was a visit we made to a Naval base in Washington. I made the trip with teammates Joe DeMaestri and Bill Renna. Being a radioman during my Navy time, I was right at home.

meeting. He looked over my papers for about 10 minutes, and then I explained the reasons I chose to jump ship — the entire story. I asked to be assigned to another ship in Portland. After quite a long meeting which included no mention of a penalty for jumping ship, he looked at me and said, "I see in your papers that you are a radio and flag signalman, and you wrote a text on the subject." I felt a bit of hope at this statement. He continued, "I want you to report to this office everyday, Monday through Friday, and teach your trade. You can live on or off base, but I can't pay you subsistence if you choose to live off base." I had some friends close by, so I chose to live off base, and received my regular pay — not a bad deal by a long shot!

Many weeks passed, and I continued to report each day, from 8:00 AM to 4:00 PM. He was a 3-stripe commander, I was a radioman 3rd class, and it was a small office — due to the close-quarters on a daily basis, he always called me by first name. I addressed him, though, as "Sir." I'm sure you're all familiar with the saying, all good things must come to an end. Unfortunately for me, that's just what happened as the commander said, "You have been here almost 30 days, and I am going to have to send you back to Treasure Island." Those sure weren't the words I was hoping to hear. I remembered earlier, he had mentioned there was an old Liberty ship that had been in port for sometime getting repairs. Turns out, it was almost ready for duty. I thought for moment, and then asked where it was headed. He said, "The South Pacific islands will be her next stop." Now this boat was a real rust-bucket, but I knew it was the best chance I had to stay away from Treasure Island, and that warrant officer. Upon my request, he assigned me to that ship. I was told that I'd be at sea for a few months. Upon completion of the mission, the ship would return to me Treasure Island, in time to play baseball. Sounds like a good deal to me, I thought. I took that baby to sea, and I spent the next 7 months taking Army supplies from the lower islands in the north to the Philippines. In fact, I was in a city called Leyte in the Philippines when President Harry Truman dropped the big bombs. I did return to Treasure Island, but only to be released from the Navy.

Needless to say, I prayed many times while in the Navy and my prayer went something like this — "If you will get me home safe from this war, let me play at least 10 years in the big leagues, and live to be 70, I will find a way to honor You." Well, I received all 3 of my requests, and have truly have tried to hold up my end of the bargain by bringing Him honor. I am proud to have served my country, and the Lord willing to tell about it.

Young men in the service can do some dumb things at times — here's one of those times. I joined a mate from the ship to hike to Manila which was 90 miles north of the bay where we were unloading Army equipment. We hitched a ride on any kind of vehicle that was heading north. Sure enough, we made it with surprising ease. The road was a supply line and was very busy on a constant basis. At that time there was quite a bit of fighting going on just outside the city. We made it there for a Saturday night liberty and headed back on Sunday. The trip back, though, turned out to be much tougher as the traffic was extremely light. It took all day Sunday to cover the 90 miles. Just as we got back to the bay where our ship was anchored, we heard the general alarm sound. We then hustled back to the ship as quick as we could. We had to get a dingy at the bay to take us back to the ship. What was happening was the Japanese were bombing the road that we had been on for those 2 days — the road to Manila. One can just imagine what could have happened had we only been halfway back to the ship. Our ship sailed from port the next day and we were back on our way to the states. The result of all of my sea time was about to pay dividends — I now had enough points to receive an honorable discharge. I only spent 3 days on the Treasure Island base before I got my orders to go to Houston, Texas, for my discharge. I received the worldly sum of $300 to buy some civilian clothes and I headed for Beaumont, Texas — the Beaumont where I had enlisted.

A Minor Experience
Playing for Burlington

I spent December of 1945 until March of 1946 in Beaumont, Texas. That had been my home for years and still was at the time. I received a notice in the mail to report to spring training with the Atlanta Crackers of the Double-A Southern Association. They were training in Gainesville, Florida. Atlanta was the club that picked up my contract after the 1942 season at Waycross, Georgia. And as I always say, baseball was sure a lot different then.

I had a good spring with the Crackers but they decided to send me to

Burlington, North Carolina. I believe it was Class-C ball of the Carolina League, however I had a Double-A contract. That meant I was making $200 dollars a month. I want you to know I thought I was cutting a fat HOG! I had made $65 a month at Waycross and $75 in the Navy. No kiddin' — I had Cadillac on my mind!

I had a good year in '46 — a batting average over .330, with 40 home runs, and knocking in more than 130. And to top that off I got myself married. I met a young lady while wintering in Beaumont and invited her to join me in Burlington. Her name was Gladys Hale.

Burlington was a great experience for me. Steve Bysco, a former catcher, was our manager and we finished in the first division. During that good season I enjoyed some of the greatest fans that could be had in minor league baseball. We played at Elon Park on the campus of Elon College. The stands held about 2,500 fans. The fans really like to gamble on a base hit, home run or a pitcher tossing a shutout. If that happened, fans would run on the field and place money in your uniform. As a player I can tell you we really liked that. Most of us only made about $200 a month and I said earlier it was pretty good money for me — you could live a lot cheaper in those days. Nonetheless, every extra dollar helped.

The club in Burlington was owned by a wealthy gentleman named Jack May. He was owner of May Hosiery Mill. One night we were playing a home game in Burlington, North Carolina. In the bottom of the first inning I came to bat and hit a home run. We led the game 1-0 until the 6th inning when Durham tied it up. The score remained tied until the bottom of the 12th inning. I came to bat with 2 out and hit a game winning home run. Needless to say, I took my time rounding the bases and exiting the field. Fans were putting money in my pockets, in my shirt or any other place they could find. When I finally got to the clubhouse, the owner of the club was standing at the door and he put a rolled up bill in my hand.

When the night has been that lucrative, all the players like to help count the evening's wages. This particular night was especially exciting as I received over $150 after the count was complete! Remember — we were only making $200 a month. When I got home to share my night's rewards with my bride Gladys, she was thrilled. Earlier, I had not added the rolled up bill that the owner had given me to my total for the evening. As I pulled it out and unrolled it I realized it was a $100 bill! I had just made $250 in one night, more than I make in a month, for hitting a pair of homers.

Four teams made up the playoffs that year. Durham, Raleigh, Burlington and Winston-Salem. We won the playoffs. If memory serves me right, I made the All-Star team, too, that year. At the end of the 1946 season I was drafted by the Cleveland Indians of the American League. I was told that this type of thing didn't happen very often. The major leagues didn't usually draft from the low minors.

The new Mrs. Zernial and I spent the winter in Texas. In March of 1947, I reported to the Cleveland Indians spring training in Tucson, Arizona. That was a big break for me to move from Class-C ball to a big league camp. I was on my way to the majors.

Before I tell you my misfortune, I want to say something about my first major league spring training. It was the first time I was meeting big league ballplayers. Lou Boudreau was the manager. Bob Kennedy and Dale Mitchell were outfielders, with Ken Keltner, Joe Gordon and Ed Robinson in the infield. Jim Hegan was behind the plate, with Bob Lemon and Bob Feller as mainstays on the mound. That group gave me first-class treatment all the way. I was really made to feel welcome to the club and I will never forget that. Three rookies on that spring roster would become fine big league players – Ray Boone, Mike Garcia and myself. The experience I received that spring, playing with that group of guys was enormous. The one thing I could do in 1946 in the Carolina League, and most of my career for that matter, was swing the bat. They made me better through helping me in the batting cage, as well as in the outfield and during the games. They were a big part of my success in the bigs. For a 24-year old country boy, that was a wanna-be big leaguer, having friends and teachers like those mentioned above is hard to put in words.

When the Indians broke camp, I felt that I had made the ballclub. As luck would have it, a turn of events was about to take place. I made a mistake, probably not my first and certainly not my last. When the club arrived in Oklahoma City for an exhibition game, I asked to leave the team to see my family in Beaumont, Texas. I would later find out that Lou Boudreau considered that a major NO-NO. While visiting in Beaumont, I received orders to report to Baltimore of the International League. I did that the very next day.

Baltimore played in a stadium designed for football, much like the Los

Angeles Coliseum. I remembered the complex because Eddie Robinson had talked with me about it while we were in spring training. He played there before he made it with the Cleveland team. I played only one game there. It was the only league in which I played that I went hitless — 0 for 4. I was happy when manager Tommy Thomas told me I was lost in the draft to the White Sox and I was headed for Hollywood.

California Here I Come
Baseball Hollywood style in 1947

The PCL was certainly a fabulous place for a kid like me to play ball. We had some great fans, especially in Hollywood and Los Angeles. Seems like there was always a very good fan base in that area — very good attendance at the ballpark which included many movie stars. You'd see Burt Lancaster, Jerry Lewis, George Raft, Cameron Mitchell, Virginia Mayo, Michael O'Shea, Dean Martin and Debbie Reynolds to name just a few. They would just be scattered among the PCL faithful, the stars often being just as big baseball fans.

During my time there I had the opportunity to work in a couple of baseball movies. They included *The Monty Stratton Story* starring Jimmy Stewart and June Allyson and The *Babe Ruth Story* starring William Bendix. That was in 1948, the same year I had the good fortune to meet the Babe himself. Frank Kelleher and I had our picture taken with him. That was really a thrill to meet such a baseball icon and one I never will forget.

The PCL at that time really had it all — great fans throughout the league and good stadiums, many of which held 20,000. We had 190 games in our schedule and played Tuesday through Sunday in each town. Travel was always by train on a Monday. The toughest trip was from Hollywood to Seattle. We played a lot of cards and poker on the way. With seven games at each stop, you would get to know your opponent pretty well. I saw the west coast from San Diego to Seattle during that time.

The Hollywood Stars had quite a background. They were originally the Salt Lake City Bees and moved to the movie capital in 1926. Based in Hollywood, they played their games at Wrigley Field, home of the Los Angeles Angels. Going way back they had some interesting characters play there

36

Here I got a chance to talk baseball with Monty Stratton during the filming of a movie made about his life — _The Monty Stratton Story._ Stewart played the lead role of Monty Stratton in the movie.

including an old spitball pitcher by the name of Frank Shellenback who was outlawed by the big leagues.

Hollywood went without a franchise in the early 1930's, but the old movie actor Fatty Arbuckle bought the Vernon Tigers and moved that team back to Hollywood where they became the Hollywood Stars. Unable to thrive, they were a bad team and sold again. This time a well-to-do restaurateur by the name of Bob Cobb bought the club. Cobb was the owner of the famous Brown Derby Restaurant. He had borrowed the money for the team from epic film director, Cecil B. DeMille, to become part owner of the team. The story goes that Mr. Cobb formed the Hollywood Baseball Association to raise money to run the team and secure a new ballpark. This was not a typical minor league board of directors as there were some notable members such as Bill Frawley of the *I Love Lucy* fame. When all the dust settled they had signed an agreement to play ball in the old Gilmore Stadium which doubled as a midget racetrack. Later came Gilmore Field where I played, which would open on May 2, 1939.

Bob Cobb was married to movie star Gail Patrick, and frequently many stars like Jack Benny, Al Jolsen, Gary Cooper and Robert Taylor were invited to throw out the first pitch at the start of the game. To make a long story short, the franchise caught on and the rest is baseball history.

Thinking of the PCL brings back some really great memories. One story I recall very well was when we had a left-hander from Cleveland — his name was Joe Krakauskas. Seattle had an outfielder by the name of Lou Novikoff. Lou just wore Joe out. Our manager Jimmie Dykes, was trying to figure a way to slow down the blistering pace at which Lou hit Joe. The answer he arrived at seemed simple enough (though not legal enough) — throw a spitter next time you face him. That's exactly what Joe tried and he threw it above Novikoff's head. Wouldn't you know it — Novikoff hit it out of the park. All Joe could say to Dykes was, "Nothing works when this guy is at the plate."

I once remember hitting a home run off Xavier Resigno, and when I got to second base he threw the rosin bag at me. Baseball is really a lot of fun.

Beside seeing movie stars, some of our PCL players actually became movie stars. Chuck Conners (*The Rifleman*) and John Berardino (*General Hospital*) were a couple of guys who had great careers in television.

Back to baseball — I really got off to a good start in the PCL with the

Hollywood Stars in '47. The team was in San Diego when my wife Gladys and I arrived in Hollywood. Not wanting to miss any opportunity, management asked me to report that day to the ball club in San Diego. They assured me they would find a place for my wife to stay until I could make my own arrangements. I had a big series in San Diego hitting several home runs and knocking in a hefty sum. Frank Kelleher was in left and Andy Skurski patrolled center for us. The club was made up of a lot of former big league players and eventually Dykes began to platoon me with Al Libke, former Cincinnati Reds outfielder who was a left-handed batter. I played in over 100 games and batted .344 for that team.

The Hollywood club of the PCL was really the beginning of my formal major league training. Being in the PCL, I was facing many former major league pitchers and competing regularly with players that had been in the bigs for many years. In those days there were guys that preferred the PCL to the major leagues. And why not — in some cases they could make more money and play in a fantastic environment up and down the west coast. Every club in the league sported rosters with quite a few ex-big league players.

At Hollywood we had Don Ross playing third and Al Unser behind the plate — both former Detroit Tigers. Frank Kelleher and Al Libke had been up with Cincinnati, and at second we had Fred Vaughn, a former Pittsburgh Pirate. It was like this on every club. I was able to gain so much baseball knowledge and experience there.

The Good Life in the PCL
1948 Hollywood Stars

The start of the 1948 season found me at spring training with the Chicago White Sox in Pasadena, California. In the final days of spring, Luke Appling and I were picking up baseballs after practice and just having some fun clowning around. Unfortunately for me the fun came to an abrupt end when I stepped on a ball and tore ligaments in my right leg. I was scheduled to open the season with the White Sox, but my injury changed everything. Our manager, Ted Lyons, said he would have to leave me in Hollywood. The injury made it impossible for me to play.

I reported to manager Jimmie Dykes and the Hollywood Stars. They were just opening their season. Dykes seemed a little perplexed as he looked at me and asked, "What can you do?" I was really walking gingerly on my right leg. I said, "Put me in right field. I might give up 5 runs, but I'll drive in 6!" I started in right field and smacked 2 home runs.

1948 in Hollywood was really my kick-off season for the big leagues. The PCL at that time covered from Seattle, Washington, in the north down to San Diego, California, in the south. Each team had numerous players with major league experience. Many fans referred to it as the third major league. If my memory serves correctly, it was a robust 189-game schedule. I played in 186 of those games and had 736 official at-bats. I tallied a league leading 236 hits with nearly 100 of the extra-base variety. I also added 156 runs driven in. This truly set me up for the majors. I was on my way to the big show along with teammates Jim Delsing and Tom Davis.

The PCL baseball fans were truly great. Kathren Scram was one of those fans, as well as a neighbor and friend of the Sims family. On one occasion she invited the Sims family to accompany her to the ballpark. Unknown to me at the time, there was a 10-year old named Marla Sims that had been part of that family outing to the ballpark. Marla's mother and father would take her to the games from time to time, and she became a real fan of mine — I guess you could say that I was sort of her favorite player. Funny how things work sometimes because as luck would have it, 12 years later I met her in Hollywood and we were married. Marla was a graduate of the Hollywood Professional School. Many of her friends went from there on to Hollywood and became stars. I met Marla in January of 1960.

One of the memorable things about Hollywood was the people that you see there. At the time, Bob Cobb was still the owner of the Brown Derby, and it was the hang-out for many of the movie industry's elite. I had the opportunity to meet so many stars of the movie world there. I guess this would be considered a little name-dropping, but those I remember most would be Jerry Lewis, Burt Lancaster, Jimmy Stewart, June Allyson, Virginia Mayo and Michael O'Shea to name a few. This was just another fringe benefit of playing ball in Hollywood — the PCL was great fun and I still see some players I know from the old days there.

In 1948 Gladys presented me with our first child, Susan Carol Zernial.

I was certainly a proud father and doing quite well in baseball. I really felt like the "King of the Hill." I had the opportunity to bring my mother to California at that time. My wife's parents, Ed and Lilly Hale, also joined us. The summer of 1948 was really a great one for me.

I knew I had a fantastic opportunity at the major league level in 1949, and I was determined to make the most of it. I did a lot of work that winter getting ready for the spring training of 1949. Knowing I was going to be reporting to the Chicago White Sox for spring training, I worked out with some really fine ball players to fine tune my skills. When you work out with guys like Hank Sauer, Peanuts Lowery, Gene Mauch and Jerry Priddy, to name just a few, you are sure to make some real progress with your baseball skills and gain valuable knowledge. We worked out mostly in Los Angeles and surrounding areas as many players wintered there. Hank Sauer and I became quite good friends.

Midway through the 1948 season, my wife and I had decided that we would make the Pacific Coast our home. We had bought our first home in Inglewood, California. Our home was right across the street from Eddie Stewart of the Chicago White Sox — really a perfect fit. It was there I spent the winter waiting for spring training with the White Sox in Pasadena, California.

On the following page I am trying to breakup a double play by sliding hard into Gene Markland at second.

MAJOR PROGRESS

I'm in the Majors Now
My first seasons in Chicago

In 1949 I completed my third spring training in a row with flying colors. In spring training for both 1947 & 1948 I had shown well, but circumstances kept me from the big leagues. In 1949 I had a good spring training with the White Sox and felt very confident about the season ahead.

Frank Lane was the general manager and our new skipper was Jack Onslow. Jack was not one of the greatest managers I'd ever played for, but he was one of the great guys in baseball. Naturally, I had to deal with Frank Lane in negotiating my contract. At the time the minimum salary in the big leagues was $5,000. It was no surprise to me when my contract offer showed up with that amount on the dotted line. As I mentioned before, life in the PCL was good and so was the money. I told him I made more than $7,000 playing in the PCL because of the long season. I asked Frank for $9,000 and we settled on $8,000, adding in a $1,000 bonus. I was off and running.

I got off to a rough start, though, and I don't mean from a performance standpoint. Heading into a game with Cleveland on May 28th I was batting at a league-leading clip of .363, but any hopes of winning a batting title would be put on hold. As fate would have it, I dove for a line drive off the bat of Thurman Tucker and I came up with the ball and a broken right collarbone. That catch would cost me 30 days in the hospital. It was a pretty serious break. Called an internal compound fracture, I had broken it in four places. Dr. Claridge was the man that gave me a choice. The first was to have a steel plate inserted — if so my career was over. The second was a procedure that offered better use of the right arm if it was successful. The choice was an easy one for me, and the procedure was performed. With lots of prayer and faith in God, I was fortunate that it was a success and I was able to continue my career.

In retrospect, my time in the hospital was not nearly as bad as I would have imagined it would be. The 30 days in Mercy Hospital in Chicago were spent on a floor with a bunch of Notre Dame and University of Illinois football players. These guys had all kinds of injuries. We were all a mess, but we had as much fun recovering as I think was possible. I was strapped down in my bed while most of the football players were in wheel chairs. That made me the central gathering point. There would be an entire group of us ball players in my room just having a good ole time. Needless to say, the nuns were not that fond of our noisy stories and late hours.

The road to recovery included many hours of rehabilitation. I saw little action the rest of the 1949 season. One highlight for me, though, was a pinch-hit home run off Joe Page of the Yankees in the top of the ninth to beat the Yanks, 10-9. I played a little in the outfield but could not throw very well. When I had to throw I would toss the ball to the outfielder next to me. Many runners took advantage of my arm by taking the extra base. It was the first time I had ever experienced a serious injury playing the game of baseball.

My rehabilitation would continue on through that winter to prepare me to be in top shape for the 1950 season. A good friend of mine, Jerry Hatfield, owned a health club in Hollywood. Jerry and I hardly missed a day of heating and stretching that right shoulder. I was more determined than ever to be ready for the 1950 campaign.

The work in the winter had paid off very well. I had a good spring with the White Sox at the Pasadena, California, spring training center. Thanks to Jerry Hatfield, the trainer, and Johnny Kerr, a White Sox scout, my right shoulder healed so completely that I could throw well from the outfield again. This was just the spark I needed — I was really excited about the coming season. After the 1949 injury had cost me a huge chunk of that season, I was ready to play ball again.

We had a pretty good club returning for the 1950 season and had high hopes of finishing in the first division. Charles Comisky, Jr., was now the president and owner of the club and Frank Lane was in his second year as the general manager. The Sox executives were expecting great things. We had some talented veterans like future Hall of Famer Luke Appling in his 20th year at shortstop, Dave Philley in center and Floyd Baker at third. They were looking for big production from me in left field as well. I had already put the pressure on myself looking to play at least 150 games of 154-game schedule. I was in only 73 games in 1949, and that simply wouldn't do for this year. As it turned out, I played a full season and hit over .280 adding 93 RBIs. To go along with that I smacked 29 home runs — at that time a new White Sox team record! This season proved in my mind that I belonged in the big leagues — I could play major league baseball.

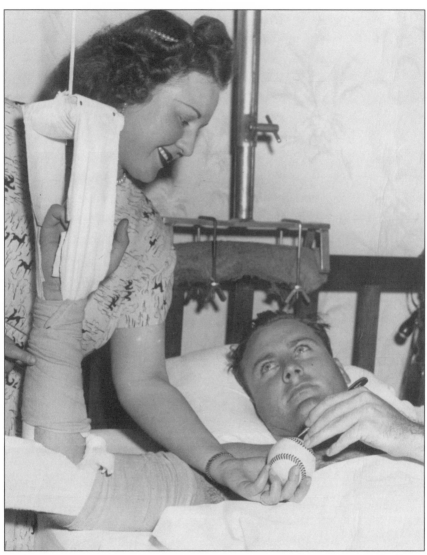

This is where I wound up after breaking my collarbone, diving for a ball against the Indians. As a photo opportunity, I am attempting to sign a ball for a fan, but being a right-hander sure limited my ability (checkout that lefty writing form.)

This is a painful shot of me scoring against the Yankees on a triple off the bat of Eddie Robinson. Unfortunately, I suffered an injury on the play.

How do you like my sliding form at third, as I hustle in against the Tribe?

Here I'm avoiding the tag at third as I slide to the outer part of the bag. Good base running and using the proper slide technique can often be the difference between winning and losing.

On the opposite page that's me with Doc Cramer, a coach with the White Sox. Doc taught me quite a lot about baseball. In his day, he was a heck of a player — he could really hit. He tallied over 2,700 hits for his career, batting just below the .300 mark.

On the down side the season proved to be a disappointing one for the team. We could not fulfill our expectation of finishing in the first division. We had a pretty good club but we just couldn't win the close ones. Nonetheless, it was my first full season and I was happy that I had finally arrived.

A Banner Season
My league leading year of 1951

In 1951, baseball began as I imagined it would, with spring training in Pasadena. I had only had an average spring training with the White Sox, as I had not hit any home runs. Looking back, it's quite odd — that was the only spring I can remember not hitting a home run. As luck would have it though, it turned out to be a fantastic power year for me! We trained at Brookside Park near the Rose Bowl. The season opened with me in a Chicago uniform, just as it had the previous 2 seasons.

Only 4 games into my 1951 season, I had gotten off to a slow start for the Sox, and in early May I was traded, along with Dave Philley, to the Philadelphia A's. Little did I know then what a fine year it was to be for me. Al Rosen of Cleveland was leading the league in homers in the early part of the season. He had 8 home runs in early May, but I almost caught him during a 4-game span. I hit 7 home runs in those 4 games — two against the New York Yankees and 5 against the St. Louis Browns. That was really an exciting run for me. The 7 home runs I hit over 4 games tied a record which is now held by several American League players. Tony Lazzeri of the Yankees set the record, and I matched him. The big league mark is held by Ralph Kiner who hit 8 home runs in 4 consecutive games. Ralph played for the Pittsburgh Pirates and was elected to the Baseball Hall of Fame.

That season we really felt we had a very talented ball club. Bobby Shantz and Alex Kellner headed up our pitching staff. Ferris Fain was at first base, Eddie Joost teamed with Pete Suder at short and second. Hank Majeski played a good portion of the year at third. Dave Philley and Elmer Valo were my teammates in the Philadelphia outfield. Unfortunately for us, the Yankees had more talent and a better club than we did. Consequently, we chased them all year and they went on to win the World Series.

Above I was a little quicker to the plate than the ball and was safe at home in game against the White Sox. Sherm Lollar was the catcher.

To the left is Alex Kellner, a fine left-hander on our A's pitching staff.

Here I am during a little celebration of the Boston Tea Party with some friends. Left to right they are Chuck Bednarik, Philadelphia Eagles' Hall of Famer, myself and Don Bollweg of the Athletics. They really could come up with some stunts in those days.

This was our Athletics' infield when I arrived in Philly. This group could really get it done defensively. From left to right: Ferris Fain, Pete Suder, Eddie Joost and Hank Majeski. When it came to twin-killings, these guys had no peers, they were tops in my book.

Jimmie Dykes was the manager when I joined the A's in 1951. He was a fine baseball man, who spent many years playing and managing for Connie Mack in Philadelphia.

Though we finished with a poor record that season, Bobby Shantz had a fine year, winning 18 and losing only 7 games. Kellner and Morrie Martin each won 11 games, with Bob Hooper adding 12 wins. I had a league leading 33 home runs, adding another circuit high 129 runs batted in. Those are bench marks for me that certainly were fulfilling. Ferris Fain led the league in batting with a robust .344 average. I had at least one home run against every team that year. No doubt, my favorite team to see in the opposing dugout that season was the St. Louis Browns — I hit 12 homers against the Brownies that year. Even with all of that offense and pitching success we didn't come close to challenging for the American League pennant in '51.

Mr. Mack had left as the manager of our club and turned the job over to Jimmie Dykes. When I was traded to the A's, Dykes was the manager. I had played for him in Hollywood of the PCL, and liked him. He enjoyed a 22-year playing career, spending all of those years between the Athletics and the White Sox. He then went on to manage both of those clubs, as well as 4 others. In 1951, the New York Yankees were the team to beat. We had some success with them because of Bobby Shantz and Alex Kellner. It was Boston and Cleveland that gave us the most problems. Cleveland had the big 4 on the mound — Bob Lemon, Bob Feller, Mike Garcia and Early Wynn. Those guys could really shut you down. For some reason, during this part of my career, two stadiums really stand out to me as legendary ball parks — Shibe Park in Philadelphia and Yankee Stadium. It's probably the names I equate with each stadium — Babe Ruth, Lou Gehrig and Miller Huggins of Yankee fame and Lefty Grove, Jimmie Foxx and Al Simmons of those fabulous A's ballclubs. Wow, those guys were amazing!

There are some memorable times for me during that banner year of mine. I had Dave Philley as my roommate, and I learned two things from him that year — snoring and cattle. It would be hard to miss the fact that Dave is a real Texan. A story comes to mind concerning Dave that involves big Luke Easter of the Cleveland Indians. He didn't like Easter because when he played first base, he often stood on top of the base. Well, one day Dave told Easter, "If you stand on top of the base again, I'm going to run right over you!" Sure enough it happened, and Dave really let him have it—Easter went about 15 feet into foul territory. When he got back to the bench, Dave said to me, "I won't do that again — I almost killed myself!" Easter weighed about 240 pounds and Dave was a solid 180-pounder. That collision knocked Easter out of that game and the following day's game. Dave didn't miss an inning — enough said.

Though the 1951 season finished rather uneventfully for our team, I felt I had really performed at a very high level. We were a second division club again, though I really felt at the time we were better than that. Looking back, it was truly a great season for me, and a fantastic baseball experience I will never forget.

A Good Season with the A's
The 1952 Philadelphia Athletics

The 1952 season in Philadelphia was a bit better than 1951 had been. Bobby Shantz had a banner year on the mound for us. That season Shantz was the best left-handed pitcher in major leagues. Winning 24 games and losing only 7, Bobby sported an earned run average of under 3.00. In addition to Shantz, Alex Kellner, Harry Byrd and Carl Scheib all finished the year posting double-figure wins. We finished in fourth place and attendance was up from the 1951 season. I mention attendance because that was such a big factor with Connie Mack and the ownership. Philadelphia was no longer a two-club city. The Philadelphia Phillies had come along with a super club in 1950, winning the National League pennant and going to the World Series. The Phillies developed such stars as Robin Roberts on the mound and Del Ennis and Richie Ashburn in the outfield.

Though we finished fourth that year, the Philadelphia fans had plenty to cheer about. Personally, I thought that year was a fine year in baseball for Philadelphia. For me, it's always a good year when you beat the Yankees in the season series, but unfortunately we couldn't top them in the league. I had another pretty good year at the plate, hitting 29 home runs and driving in 100 runs. Ferris Fain hit American League pitching at a .327-clip to claim the second of his 2 batting crowns. Eddie Joost and Dave Philley put together good years, but I felt Pete Suder was beginning to feel his age. The A's opted to bring in Hall of Famer George Kell's younger brother to play second. Named Skeeter Kell, he never matched the skills of brother George, but then

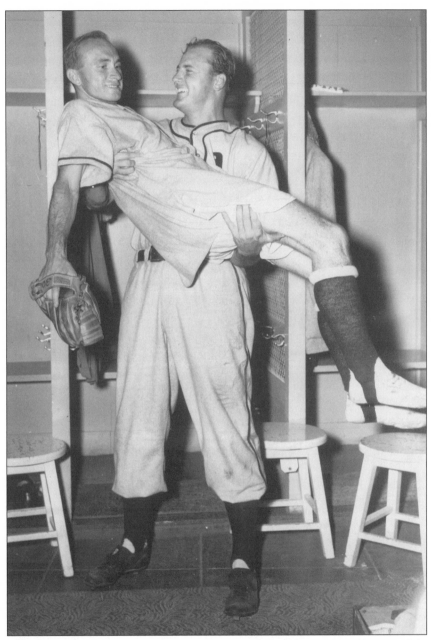

Here I am holding Bobby Shantz after he shutout the Yankees for his 13th victory of the season. The shutout was tossed at Yankee Stadium and he blanked them 12-0.

again, not many did.

The real talk of the team that year — and of the league, for that matter was Bobby Shantz. He stood about 5'-7" and weighed all of about 140 pounds. Beside his 24 victories, he pitched in the All-Star Game and was the American League MVP. It was truly a pleasure to play behind Bobby the days he was on the hill. Bobby always kept you in the game because he was always on the mound and ready to pitch — you had to be ready to go. Very seldom was a successful bunt executed when Shantz was pitching with Ferris Fain at first. Bobby won 8 gold gloves and would have won more, but the award didn't begin until the late 1950s. Fain was a great fielder as well, and between the two there wasn't much opportunity for safely bunting your way on base.

The signing of contracts was not a big deal in those days. Players didn't have agents to negotiate, and the simple truth was you got what you could get. After the 1951 season, when I led the league in home runs and RBIs, Earle Mack and Roy Mack gave me a substantial raise, don't get any ideas though — nothing compared to today's players, but when I almost duplicated my season of 1951 in '52 I was given a cut. I was told I didn't have as good a year as in 1951 — go figure.

Seems several fist-fights or team brawls take place every year between clubs in the heat of battle. One such brawl that I specifically recall was while I was with the Athletics when we were playing the Chicago White Sox. Saul Rogovin was pitching for the White Sox in the bottom of the 12th inning in Philadelphia and the game was knotted at 1-1. Elmer Valo was on first with 2 outs. I was dug in at the plate and Rogovin rifled a fastball right down the middle of the plate. I swung and tagged it, hitting the left-centerfield wall with my blast. Gus Niarhos was the Sox catcher and Valo, our runner at first, wasn't called "The Bull" for nothing. Well, somewhere along the way Valo decided he could score from first, and as he rounded third it was pretty clear he was going to be out by 15 feet. Gus received the relay throw and was blocking the plate. Valo never slowed and nailed Niarhos, knocking him out. Niarhos dropped the ball and Valo was safe. What took place after that was a big league brawl.

Rogovin grabbed Valo, who was also knocked out with a big gash over his eye where he hit the mask of Niarhos, and began punching him. I was running in from second base to help out when I saw Ferris Fain, fly in mid-

That's me up top, posing with our big puncher, Ferris Fain, during spring training.

To the right is "The Bull," Elmer Valo, who always lived up to his nickname.

At times, you have to slide hard to score — see the ball on ground. Catcher is Sammy White of Boston, and the collision knocked the ball loose and I was safe.

air, and plant a straight left directly on the nose of Rogovin. Saul had a big nose to begin with, and that punch didn't do anything to help it out — you should have seen it after the fight. As with most fights, many were involved, but the most damage had already been done with the collision at home plate — though the punch by Fain was a close second. I happened to be the peacemaker in this one. Talk about a bang-bang finish — and I mean literally!

A Tough Season in Philadelphia
The 1953 Philadelphia Athletics

This was a season that was total disaster for the Mack family. We lost almost 100 games — 95 to be exact. That meant we only posted 59 wins. A modest 362,000 was all the paid attendance for that season. Somehow both Eddie Robinson at first and myself still had productive years. Robinson hit 22 home runs and added 102 RBIs. I hit behind Robbie and hit 42 homers while knocking in 108. Dave Philley led the club in hitting with a .303 batting mark.

Bobby Shantz suffered a broken wrist on his pitching arm and only pitched 16 games. He was only able to tally 5 wins for the season. Compare that with the 1952 season when he won 24 and was the MVP. Alex Kellner and Harry Byrd led the staff with 11 wins each. We could only muster a 7th-place finish in the American League. It was Joe DeMaestri's first year, taking over for Eddie Joost, and he had a good season. Joe and I became good friends that year and remain so to this day.

The Philadelphia Phillies, who also played at Connie Mack Stadium, continued to play great ball after winning the pennant in 1950. The Philadelphia fans went in their direction for the most part. We still had some very loyal fans, and from that was born the Philadelphia Athletics Historical Society years later.

Connie Mack was hoping our 1953 team would bring him and the club back in to prominence in the American League. Unfortunately, it was not meant to be. He was out of money, and things had gotten pretty tight. Selling the ballclub was talked about on a regular basis in those days. As a player you knew that the more this type of talk surfaced, the more likely it was to actually take place.

During this season, Ferris Fain was traded to the White Sox for Eddie Robinson — a trade which turned out to be good trade for both clubs. I was voted to be the starting left fielder for the American League All-Star team. The game was played in Cincinnati. Eddie Robinson was also chosen to play. The American League was on the losing end in this one but, I did get the first base hit — a single off Philadelphia ace, Robin Roberts.

The Final Season in Philly
1954 Philadelphia Athletics

It had all started during the 1951 season in Philadelphia — baseball, as in the Athletics, was on the ropes. The Philadelphia Phillies had taken over the majority of the fan base in the city. In 1954, our attendance was just a little above the 300,000 mark. We had some fine, loyal fans left, but not nearly enough to keep the ballclub alive. We lost 103 games that year which didn't do anything to improve our standing with the avarage fan in the city. Although Philadelphia fans can be tough, let's face it — not many fans in any city enjoy a team losing that much.

I broke my left shoulder in June of '54, and was out a month. I was still able to lead the club in RBIs with 62. That said, we still had some guys that could really hit the ball. Bill Renna, Vic Power, Bill Wilson — rookie Jim Finigan led the club in batting boasting a solid .302 average.

Most of the year the players knew that the club was going to be sold. Maybe that wasn't the entire explanation, but it had a lot to do with our team's play on the field. Eddie Joost had taken over for Jimmie Dykes as the manager. Jimmie never really had any sort of magic touch in putting a good team on the field, so changing managers made no difference. We were just a bad ballclub at this point.

There seemed to be some rumbling in the front office amongst the Macks. Earle and Roy, as I had heard, didn't agree on much of anything. I am sure a lot of pressure was being put on all of the Macks to sell the club and let the move occur. In the four years I was with the team, the best attendance for one season was just over 600,000, and that was in 1952 — Bobby Shantz's big year with 24 wins and league MVP honors. The word I had gotten was that the

Solid contact feels great — I mean when you really get a hold of one. Here I am getting that feeling as I clout one against Yankees. The catcher is Hall of Fame player, Yogi Berra.

Here I am with Eddie Joost, picking uniforms for spring training. Those were the good old days and I sure enjoyed my time on the diamond.

Here I am sliding home safely after I tripled earlier in the inning. The Detroit catcher is Joe Ginsberg.

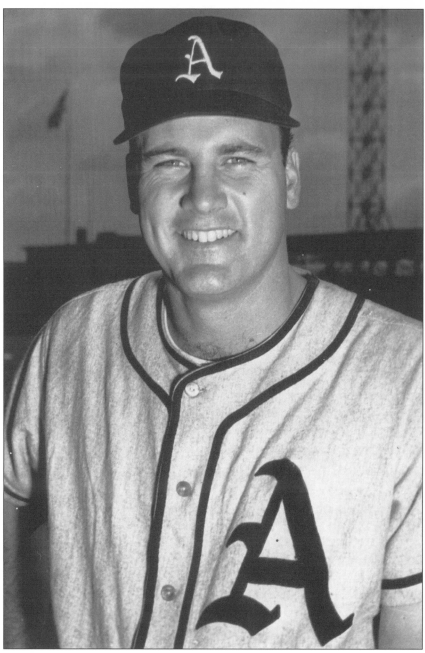

I hope it comes across in this picture just how happy I was playing ball for a living.

pressure was put on the Mack family to sell the club to Arnold Johnson — who you might say was a close friend of the Yankees. Then the club would be moved to Kansas City, Missouri.

Sure enough, that proved to be a fact. Going back to the early 1930's the Philadelphia Athletics put it to the Yankees for league championships. Those were the great days of Robert "Lefty" Grove, Rube Walberg and Chief Bender on the mound. Jimmie Foxx, Al Simmons, Mickey Cochrane — and so many more Philly greats. Philadelphia was not that many miles south of Yankee Stadium and the Bronx Bombers. Who could forget the Yanks who had the mighty Babe, Lou Gehrig and many more star players. So maybe it's payback time — who knows?

Many of the players who had experienced great years in Philadelphia may not have looked forward to moving — Bobby Shantz, Alex Kellner, catcher Joe Astroth and myself. For some of the players, however, I'm sure the move was a positive thing. For me personally, it was quite sad at the end of the season, saying good-bye to the fans and friends alike. Little did we know that years later the Philadelphia Athletics Historical Society would form and we'd once again see many old familiar faces. I never saw Connie Mack Stadium again — only pictures of it being torn down. I have great memories of the house that Foxx, Grove and Simmons built under the greatest legend of all time, Cornelius McGillicuddy.

The 1954 season was a disaster in so many ways. The attempt to recover from such a bad season that was 1953 was, at best, going to be extremely difficult. I am reluctant to tell this part of 1954 but feel it's necessary.

Eddie Joost was made manager of our '54 squad. Looking back, some of the players didn't want to play for Eddie. I don't know all of the facts, but as I recall Eddie Robinson and Dave Philley asked to be traded. They didn't want to play for Eddie. I had played a couple years against Eddie, and while I had no run-ins with him, apparently some did. When I joined the team in 1951, Eddie was our shortstop. As a leadoff man, he would hit 20 home runs and drive in a lot of runs as well. To me, he was a fine leadoff hitter as well as good teammate. In 1954, however, things began to change. He saw very limited playing time, only appearing in a few ball games. In my opinion, if they wanted Eddie to manage just for that final season, he should have been a playing manager.

Breaking-up the double play is your job when you're on at first. Here I am sliding into Gil McDougald of the Yankees, trying to make his job a little tougher.

We got off to a terrible start and the club was in complete turmoil. Players were grumbling and we couldn't win at all. I was off to a fair start, but Eddie had to blame the losses on someone. That someone turned out to be me. Then a day came that I will always regret, but it happened nonetheless. Eddie had penciled me hitting 6th in the lineup, but it didn't bother me until one of the umpires said to me, "What's Eddie got against you?" When I heard those words I got a bit hot under the collar and a few words were exchanged between Eddie and myself. The argument that ensued put us in the front office with Roy and Earle. Eventually things were settled between Eddie and myself. Then in June, playing in Philadelphia, we we're getting blasted 18-0. It was towards the end of the game and I dove for a line drive off the bat of Billy Consolo. The dive broke my right shoulder, and that finished the year for me — the A's, unfortunately, were already done.

Eddie Joost may not have been the manager that many had hoped for, but he was a fine baseball player. Since the incident in 1954, he and I became friends. After retirement, Eddie and I have made several trips to the A's Historical Society functions together and played golf in the same tournaments. We never speak of the altercation — it's just part of the game of baseball.

Kansas City Here We Come
The 1955 Kansas City Athletics

The Philadelphia Athletics were bought by Arnold Johnson and Co. then moved to Kansas City, Missouri. Spring training still took place in West Palm Beach, Florida. A few players did not make it to Kansas City, but most were at spring training. We were all anxious to complete spring training so we could fly to Kansas City. We all heard about the big welcome parade that was planned — and that's just what happened. Thousands welcomed us, and I can remember that we all felt pretty good about it. We were now officially the Kansas City Athletics. Unfortunately, we were still the '54 Philadelphia ballclub on the field — and we played like it. Instead of 300,000 fans, though, we played before an amazing 1,400,000 in our new home.

All kidding aside, we did have a pretty talented team. Vic Power at first, Hector Lopez at second, Joe DeMaestri at shortstop and Jim Finigan rounded out the infield at third. Joe Astroth, a real veteran backstop, was behind the plate. The outfield on this club became manager Lou Boudreau's project, though. We had six pretty good outfielders including Bill Renna, Enos Slaughter, Elmer Valo, Bill Wilson, Harry Simpson and myself. Boudreau just about went off his rocker using a two-platoon system that he liked. I could easily elaborate for a few chapters on Lou's managing. He seemed to get fairly good production on the field, but it just didn't translate to wins at the end of the game. We lost 91 games that year. We used 26 regulars and 22 pitchers during the season. I was the only outfielder to get over 400 at-bats, 413 to be exact, and managed to hit 30 home runs. It was second to Mantle's 37 round-trippers.

At times the fans were more enjoyable to watch than the team on the field. I'll tell you this, though — I had never played before a more enthusiastic bunch of fans. They were with us every step of the way. I had a fan club that wore letters on their sweaters spelling out Z-E-R-N-I-A-L. I was a guest at many of their parties and I don't think they missed a game. It was fantastic!

Kansas City had a number of perks for the new Athletics that had come to town — not the least of which was TWA. The TWA hostess home base was there. You can bet our single guys went wild. There were several that got married. I am not really sure about this, but I believe Enos Slaughter found his fourth wife among that TWA group. I am sure many of the young ladies attended games. We were second in the league in attendance that season, another huge Kansas City benefit. I still have friends that I made there, and stay in contact with them to this day. The city was not known as a night-life town, but it boasted some of the finest steak houses in the land — Majestic Steak House and the Shrimp King, to name a couple.

I think the fans in Kansas City should have a book written about them — I know I'd buy it. The first year totaled 1,400,000, followed in 1956 and 1957 by an average of over 1,000,000 — and we were a losing team. Our upside was that we had players the fans enjoyed watching. I can't praise our fans any more than to say they were great! Off the field we had a couple of incidents happen, but nothing the club couldn't take care of.

I believe that if I played more in 1955 I could have driven in 100 runs and perhaps led the league in home runs. Unfortunately, Lou Boudreau was dead-set on his two-platoon system. As I said before, he had the players to do

Here I am holding my favorite piece of lumber — a 36 inch long, 36 ounce bat. I sure enjoyed putting one of these to good use.

it. I liked being in Kansas City. Our travel was much better as we now had charter flights to each city. No more trains — that was a blessing. We were flying on United Airlines charter flights, and I remember our captain was Bud Jordan. The planes were small like DC-3's and Convairs. For those of you that don't remember, those were dual-prop planes that didn't carry much of a payload. Later, we really thought we had moved up in the world when we flew on some four-prop planes.

I remember one trip, leaving Boston and flying to Kansas City. I believe we were boarding a twin-engine Convair. Captain Jordan suggested that five of the players wait for the next plane, but not one player volunteered to wait. The captain knew we were overloaded, but we all boarded. The only seat left was the jump seat with the pilot and co-pilot. Bud Jordan was a friend of mine, so I didn't mind my seat at all. We took our position for take-off.

Now, the runway ended at the bay, and even with a small plane you needed the majority of runway for a safe take-off. About the time we reached take-off speed, Jordan pulled back to climb and left the ground but simply stayed level, no lift at all. We all knew at that point we were overloaded. The captain now throttled for more speed, and he tried again with the same results — no lift. Now things started to get a little exciting. We were quickly reaching the point of no return. I was then standing and hanging on for dear life. We were wide open and coming up on the end of the runway and the bay fast! A thousand thoughts were going through my mind. I'm sure the pilots were thinking many of the same things I was. The airplane was shaking like it was on a bumpy road. I was really hanging on as we came to the end of the runway. Suddenly we were over water with same problem — no lift. We also had a new issue approaching. We were heading straight towards a small mountain. The way I saw it there were only 2 options — dunk in the water or fly right into the side of the mountain.

As we approached the mountain and a mountain road, we felt a lift. With that, Captain Jordan was able to bank the plane to the left and make the turn around the mountain. What a amazing job he did getting us through that. There was a moment of silence and I said to Bud, "I didn't think we were gonna make it." Bud answered back, "Neither did I."

After we settled down on our flight, I asked Bud his thoughts. He said he knew we were in real trouble at the point of no return and he figured he would just fly off the end of the runway if he had to and pancake into the bay. Since we didn't settle down any he knew we were getting some lift, but not enough to bank to the left. His next thought was to fly toward the mountain, hoping to get an updraft of air. That is exactly what happened and we all lived to see another day. We all owe one to Captain Jordan for that day — he saved a lot of lives with his flying ability. He must still be around today. I wish I knew how to reach him — I'd thank him again!

As far as baseball goes for that season, I have some idea of what Boudreau's managing plans were. Unfortunately, they weren't successful. As I said before, we had some pretty good talent, but we didn't have a good team. On a good note, we didn't have any more exciting take-offs by plane and the traveling was great. In fact, some of the plane rides were more pleasurable than our games, though I will say I truly enjoyed playing games in old Municipal Stadium. It remains a true landmark in my mind on my baseball journey.

From City to City

1956-57 Kansas City Athletics & 1958-59 Detroit Tigers

The 1956 Kansas City A's were just about as bad as '54 Philadelphia Athletics. The bad news was we lost 102 games in 1956 (in Philly we lost 103), but the good news was that we had 700,000 more fans watch us in Kansas City. We had some pretty solid ball players. Lou Boudreau just didn't know how to win with them.

Our infield was well above average with Vic Power at first base. He batted .309 with 40 extra-base hits. Jim Finigan, Joe DeMaestri and Hector Lopez, all skilled players, rounded out that group. The outfield could have produced more, but, there again, Boudreau used his two-platoon system. Lou Skizas and Harry Simpson hit over .300. Trouble was Bill Renna, Enos Slaughter and myself just couldn't get in enough games. Pitching was an issue, too, as we didn't seem to be able to perform at a consistently high level. Our mainstays on the mound that year were Shantz, Keltner and Ditmar, and they only posted 21 wins between them. Shantz was used mainly in relief.

The 1957 season was about the same. Billy Hunter was acquired to play second base and Hector Lopez was moved to third. He replaced Jim Finigan who was traded. We struggled again as a team and could only muster a 7th place finish in the league. Lou Boudreau was fired in the middle of the season and Harry Craft took over as the skipper. I didn't get to play at all in the early going, but once Craft took over I played a more and was able to be more productive.

I've got to tip my cap to the Kansas City fans during those three years. They really stood by us through thick and thin. I believe we had enough talent on the field to win more games in my three years there, but it didn't happen. I will say it again, I will always remember the fans in Kansas City. To be more specific, I recall one of our faithful so well that I still communicate with her to this day. Her name is Nancy Morris. Her mother and aunt brought her to the ballpark almost every day. She loved the Kansas City Athletics and collected the autograph of each player for every season. Now that's a devoted fan you can count on!

At the end of the 1957 season I was traded to the Tigers. I spent all winter thinking of Detroit. They had a team that would be in contention and I thought they wanted me to play on a regular basis. In the outfield they had Al Kaline in right and Harvey Kuenn in center. I had the chance to be the regular left fielder. Frank Lary, Jim Bunning and Paul Foytack were the heart of the pitching rotation.

When it was contract time, I dealt with former major league player John McHale. He was the acting general manager for the ball club. McHale had played briefly in the majors but hadn't produced much. At that time in Detroit, though, he was the man. This is where I think playing for Boudreau in Kansas City was costly for me.

I had averaged 25 home runs a season in Kansas City on a part-time basis. When McHale sent me a contract, it was complete with a cut in pay. I was not satisfied with this offer at all, and challenged him on that. His response, "Not bad money for a part-time player." I didn't contest the contract or the comment, but in retrospect I should have. Seems I had my fair share of trouble with former ballplayers in those days.

Spring training was in Lakeland, Florida. I had a good spring and felt I had a great shot to be in the outfield on opening day. Our home season opener in Detroit was against the Cleveland Indians with over 46,000 in attendance. Herb Score took the hill for the Tribe and Billy Hoeft was our starter. I was in left, Harvey Kuenn was in center and Al Kaline patrolled right. Our manager was Jack Tighe. I hit a triple that day, and thought I had it all figured out this time — I would be in left field. Unfortunately, it didn't work out that way. Charlie Maxwell, a good left-handed hitter became the regular left fielder. I played in only 24 games in the outfield in 1958. We had a good ballclub that year and were picked to give the Yankees a run for their money. I went to bat only 124 times but hit a healthy .323 and led the league in pinch hitting, with 15 pinch hits. One of those was my 10th career pinch homer, which at that time was a record. We played about .500 baseball that year and finished in fifth place.

Let me tell you a little more about John McHale. Even though I didn't agree with how he handled my contract, McHale went on to make quite a name for himself in baseball. In 1959 he became general manager of the Braves, a position he held until 1966. Today, McHale serves as president of the Association of Professional Baseball Players of America, and is a member of the Baseball Hall of Fame board of directors. His son is president and CEO of the Tigers in Detroit. The McHale family has certainly been able to climb the ladder of success in baseball. However, I will always feel he made a less than complimentary remark to me when I signed with Detroit in 1958. He was correct about my part-time player status, but Kansas City had dictated that — it was out of my control.

I signed again in 1959 with the Tigers. McHale had moved on to greener pastures and there was no cut in salary this time, although in my estimation there was not much left to cut. I felt that between the Detroit Tigers and the Kansas City Athletics, I had really been hit hard financially.

Jimmie Dykes was hired as manager when Bill Norman was fired. Norman had replaced Tighe during the '58 season. I had played for Dykes many times before, but this time I was not his favorite player. About the only bright spot for me in 1959 was when Dykes came to me one day and asked if I could play first base. Our two first basemen were Gail Harris and Larry Osborne. I answered Dykes with a confident quickness, "I am the best first baseman in the league." What else was I going to say? I wanted to play. I saw action in 32 games at first, hit 7 home runs and drove in 26. That became the end of the trail for me as a player. In June of that year I turned 37 years of age and no longer fit into any ballclub's plans. Like many players, the decision to retire was not an easy one, but I thought it was time — I retired from baseball.

My Career's Demise in a Nut Shell
Injury often signals the end

My first 6 seasons in the American League, 2 with the Sox in Chicago and 4 with the Athletics in Philadelphia, were very productive years for me. I was extremely satisfied with my production, both at the plate and in the field. Unfortunately, the beginning of the end began far too soon for me. If I had to put my finger, on the point that my big league career was starting to fade, I'd say it was when I broke my right shoulder on June 8, 1954, in Philadelphia. We were playing against the Boston Red Sox, and I would play very little the rest of the '54 season.

Connie Mack sold the club to Arnold Johnson and we were moving to Kansas City, Missouri. Lou Boudreau had been named manager. I had good spring training and we were set for our opening in Kansas City. The fans gave us a great welcome, really turning out to see us play. We performed relatively well, but still played well under .500 baseball. Fortunately, I had fully recovered from the broken shoulder of 1954. Unfortunately, Boudreau was the type of manager that liked to use the two-platoon player system, and this was going to cost me quite a bit of playing time.

He had some good outfielder talent with which to work his platoon strategy. I would estimate that it worked for him about 25% of the time. Using Enos Slaughter, Elmer Valo, Bill Renna, Suitcase Simpson and myself, we pulled from an arsenal of pretty good left and right-handed batters. This cut in playing time was difficult for me and affected my production drastically. Here's a fine example. In 1955 I only went to bat 410 times, hitting 30 home runs and driving in nearly 90 runs. I must have missed the opportunity to play in 25 to 30 games due to the platoon system. One could only assume that had I played on a regular basis my numbers would have been considerably better. Mantle led the league in home runs with 37 that year. My numbers compare favorably to Mantle if you average them out over another 25 or so games. It was really hard for me to figure — I am putting up Mantle-like numbers for that season and not playing full-time. It seemed obvious enough to me — Lou didn't like me much as a player. It's really tough to sit out games when you are having a productive season and you have the numbers to back it up, but that's right where I was. You might ask, "What about Slaughter — he's a Hall of Famer?" Enos was at the end of a fine career, and so was Elmer Valo. At the time I really gave a lot of thought about asking to be traded. That was just not in the cards for me, though — I was just not that kind of guy.

I really thought that 1956 would be better. I couldn't have been more wrong as it was worse. I played much less than in the previous season. I really thought that this system was not only hurting me, but the entire ball club. Though I did not air my thoughts to everyone, I did talk with Harry Craft. He was one of our coaches and a very fine center fielder in his day. Harry and I had many a conversation about Boudreau's two-platoon system. For what it was worth, Harry agreed with me. That was little consolation, though, as 1956 season was a totally lost season for me. I got less than half of the at bats I would typically get, which only translated to 16 home runs for the year.

I was offered a contract for the 1957 season and I gave a lot of thought about playing that year. I felt I was too young to retire, so I decided to report to spring training. I just hoped I would be given the opportunity that I believed was due me. In the past, I felt then as I still do today, that my full season statistics speak for themselves. I was regularly among the league leaders in numerous offensive categories when given the entire season to perform. If given the same chance I felt confident I would deliver. As fate would have it, however, the season got started and life on the Athletics was about the same. If I were as outspoken then as I am today, there would have certainly been some colorful fireworks!

As they say, "One man's pleasure is another man's pain." Those words rang true in the 1957 season. Lou Boudreau's misfortune was a break for me. In my estimation, Lou had done a lousy job managing the team. He was fired in the early going and Harry Craft was signed to manage in his place. Harry sat down with me and we talked about my situation. I had lost large parts of 2 seasons with Boudreau. Craft installed me in as the regular left fielder and I responded with 27 home runs and nearly 70 RBIs in a little over 400 at bats. Unfortunately, I did not hit for a good average. At the end of the '57 season the front office decided to shake things up a bit. Harry went on to coach elsewhere and I was dealt to Detroit. So my days with Kansas City had come to an end. I had played a total of 7 years with the Athletics.

I really looked forward to going to Detroit. It brought back many memories of my childhood, as I had followed the Tigers when I lived in Beaumont, Texas. The Double-A minor league, Beaumont Exporters were a farm club of the Tigers. As mentioned earlier, general manager John McHale, a so-so player during his career, cut my salary — I accepted the cut and decided I would produce with the bat. After a productive season I would simply ask for the salary cut back. I was determined to make the Detroit club, and I did in 1958. I opened in left field with Harvey Kuenn in center and Al Kaline in right, and now I was back in the game. Though the year was not what I hoped, I did lead the league in pinch-hitting. I also set a new record at that time with my 10th pinch-hit home run. I hit that one off of Baltimore pitcher Billy O'Dell. Once again though I had been relegated to bench jockey. Unfortunately, McHale was right when I talked with him about a contract and being part-time.

I went back to play with Detroit in 1959. Knowing the way '58 had turned out, I had a pretty good idea that this was going to be my last season. I performed satisfactorily through some stretches, but not how I was used to playing. It was my last year in the bigs.

In hindsight, this is why I point to that shoulder injury as the beginning of my end. After that season there would be no more 500-plus at-bats in a season or 145-plus games patrolling the outfield. I can't help but think that if I had been given the opportunity to continue to play full-time in the years after my injury, my baseball career would have been even more productive than it was.

The photo on the opposite page shows me catching for Marilyn Monroe as Joe Dobson looks on. This was a publicity photo shoot set up by Marilyn's agent. They made the rounds to numerous locations looking for photo opportunities, and we were all happy that we qualified as one of the stops.

DIAMOND STORIES

Marilyn & Joe

A Hollywood and baseball experience

In 1951, the Chicago White Sox opened spring training at Brookside Park in Pasadena, California. I think we were about 10 days into camp when a group of agents and photographers showed up at the ball park. They had a very beautiful young lady with them for a photo session. It didn't take long for all to recognize it was a new starlet by the name of Marilyn Monroe.

At the time, Miss Monroe had only made a few films and was not yet the superstar she was soon to become. Her agent was out to get her all the publicity he could, and today just happened to be baseball day. Joe Dobson, Hank Majeski and myself were asked to have our pictures taken with Marilyn. As you may have already guessed, we all jumped at the idea. Hundreds of pictures were taken, including quite a few with me. Several magazines ran nice picture spreads that we all enjoyed. It seems to me that *Esquire Magazine* had the most pictures, and many involved me. Marilyn was not only blessed with beauty from head to toe, but was also a very intelligent person. Contrary to some folks' beliefs, she was not just another pretty blond. Marilyn was single at the time, but, she had been married to a Navy man.

It was that year that Joe DiMaggio was completing his last season in the pinstripes of the Bronx Bombers. That summer I had been traded to the Philadelphia Athletics and we were in New York to play the Yankees. Joe was in centerfield for New York and I was in left for the A's. Unknown to me, Marilyn Monroe was in New York promoting one of her movies. Earlier, Joe had made the comment, "Why should a bush-leaguer like Zernial get to meet her when I have not." This comment was referring to the picture layout that appeared in many magazines of the day.

Well, leave it to the baseball writers — they got wind of that story and put their own spin on the facts. Joe got the introduction to Marilyn, but the writers released a story reporting that I had introduced the two. It had happened indirectly, but not as the writers said. To this day that story still stands. Joe, until the day he passed away, believed I told that story and that I perpetuated it thereafter.

I believe it was 1954 when they married, and the rest is history. Later,

That's me walking to the field in spring training with Marilyn Monroe during our photo shoot. Life in the big leagues sure had its perks some days.

when I would see Joe at golf tournaments or other functions, he would ignore me. He was always was very uncomplimentary of me. All that aside, he did know that I knew Marilyn before he had. Later, I was fortunate enough to meet a young lady from that same group in Hollywood. Her name was Marla Sims, and I convinced her to change her name to Zernial. We are still together, and it just may be that for once I outdid Big Joe. Though Joe made it known what he thought of me through his books, it's good to know, I was involved with two legends — Joe and Marilyn.

I enjoyed many of her movies and played against one of the greatest in centerfield — it was truly a situation I was glad to be in. Both are gone now, and I will always believe she might have been a victim of foul play — but that's another story.

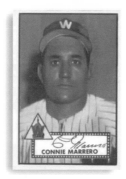

Long Bats & Long Balls

The Connie Marrero story

I am recalling a story I told about former Athletics outfielder Al Simmons. The Hall of Famer gave me one of his bats, telling me that it was long enough to reach that big slider that Bob Lemon threw. That slider helped put Lemon in baseball's Hall of Fame. I recall using that same bat off another pitcher that had a great slider, Connie Marrero. He pitched for the Washington Senators of the American League. Connie was from Venezuela, stood about 5'-7" and was very stocky.

I was with the Philadelphia Athletics at the time, and we were hosting the Senators. Marrero was on the mound. I got this story from a baseball fan

Speaking of Joe DiMaggio, that's him on the right chasing a triple I hit in Yankee Stadium. Check out the 457 Ft. sign — you had to really hit it back in those days to leave the yard in the Bronx when you went to center. They have slowly moved the wall in over the years making the centerfield wall much more inviting these days.

that knows Marrero very well and talks him often in Venezuela. I went to the plate with this wagon tongue, as the bat was called. Al Simmons used a bat that was 39 inches long and weighed 39 ounces. To give you some idea how big this bat was, my normal bat was 36 inches and weighed 36 ounces and that was considered a big bat. The average bat today, weighs about 32 ounces and is only 34 inches long.

Well, I used this wagon tongue against pitchers that used the slider, more often than any other pitch, and there were several in the league. When you faced Marrero, 8 out of 10 pitches would be the slider, and he had outstanding control of that pitch. When I got to the plate, Marrero took a long look at me and the bat I was using. He kind of looked at the stands and then to the sky, as if to say, "What do I do?" He knew his slider was his best pitch. He gave me his best pitch and I launched it into the upper deck in Philadelphia for a home run. When I circled the bases and reached home plate, there was Marrero, holding my bat and telling the umpire that it was illegal. This is not just a funny story, it also illustrates the many mind games that are constantly occurring during a baseball game. Just a small part of what makes the game so wonderful to me.

The Catch

Al "Zeke" Zarilla's impossible grab

Many players have made great plays in the outfield over the years. You may recall the catch made in center by Willie Mays on a long drive off the bat of

Vic Wertz at the Polo Grounds in the World Series. Who could forget Al Gionfriddo's snag of Joe DiMaggio's shot in the leftfield corner and DiMaggio's quick kick of the ground in disappointment. Maybe you saw the diving catch made by Ron Swoboda, also in the World Series. I could go on and on, but I want to tell you about the greatest catch I believe was ever made — and it never made the news.

It came in an exhibition game when the National League All-Stars were up against the American League All-Stars. These teams were put together by the great tennis player, Bobby Riggs. That's right — the same Bobby Riggs who once challenged Billie Jean King in a tennis match and lost. We were playing in San Diego, California. It was a very close game and we were tied, 2-2, going into the 6th inning. It was just about that time, as fate would have it, that the fog rolled in. The fog can come in quickly and heavily, as many of you probably know in San Diego. I was playing leftfield and Al Zarilla was in right. The fog was very thick and close to the ground. Anything hit in the air was tough to see and likely to become an adventure. On ground balls you could make a play with much less difficulty.

As the innings progressed it got worse. I really thought the game might be called, but some how we got to the bottom of the 9th inning. The National League was at bat with two on and two out. Slugger Duke Snider of the Brooklyn Dodgers came to the plate. With fog situation you could still see the field of play, but not much else. The pitch was made and I saw Duke take this mighty left-handed swing. I thought from my position in leftfield that the ball was gone. I watched Zarilla going back to the fence, leaping against the wall and making a one-handed catch. It was an amazing circus catch, the likes I had never seen before or seen since. From my view I was sure it was outta here. Well, when we got to the dugout I said to Zeke, "How did you make that catch?" Al answered with a grin, "I have been carrying a ball in my pocket for 2 innings — I never saw the ball Duke hit. I just took the ball out of my pocket and made it look like a great play." Snider put up a big beef with the umpire who had called him out, but he lost. The score remained tied going to the 10th inning and the game was called due to the fog. In my book, that was the greatest play I ever saw made in the outfield!

Triples Can Be Tough
Albie Pearson said a mouthful

This is a story I heard about a young outfielder that came up to the Washington Senators in 1958. The outfielder's name — Albie Pearson. He was not a big man, as outfielders go in the big leagues, but he had a big heart and plenty of desire which made up for any size constraints. I met Albie towards the end of my career with Detroit when he came to the major leagues. Pearson stood 5'-5" and weighed in at about 140 pounds. He was a factor in many games with his baseball skills and knowledge. He played 9 years in the majors, ending his career with the California Angels.

The story I heard went something like this. I am not sure of the opponent, but Pearson, at the time, was with the Angels. The first time at bat, he hit a ball down the first base line and saw that he had a chance for a triple. Completing his charge for third, he slid into the bag, thinking he had the beat the throw. Unfortunately, the umpire, about 6'-4", didn't quite see it that way and shouted, "Your out!" Pearson glared up at him because he thought he was safe.

A few innings later, Pearson is at the plate again. This time he lines a ball to right center, rounds first and second and heads for third again. This time he knows he has the play beat, sliding hard and standing up to brush himself off. He looks at the huge umpire with a quite serious look, and the umpire says, "Your out!" This time he stares at the umpire, giving him a long look. Remember, in baseball you not only need the talent to play, but you also need the ability be quick thinking, too. Now, up for the third time, Pearson hits the ball to left-center and has the play right in front of him. He sees his chance for a triple and heads for third, sliding in with no doubt of his safety, beating the throw. The big umpire standing right over him says, "You're out."

That was the last straw — it was all Albie could take. He leaps right up, seeming to reach the umpire's belt buckle. Pearson is really giving it to the big umpire. Now remember, you have to be quick thinking in this game. Well, at this point the umpire has finally had enough of Pearson's tongue, and with a loud voice exclaims, "Get out of here or I'll bite your head off." Pearson, using his quick wit, said to the ump, "If you do, you would have more brains in your stomach than you have in your head."

Albie Pearson had a very successful major league baseball career, and after retirement studied the ministry and is pastor of a church in California.

A Less Than Routine Single

The longest single I ever hit

It was a hot afternoon at Fenway Park, a real blistering day in Boston. The great Ted Williams was patrolling left field with Dom DiMaggio in center, and Al Zarilla handling right. Vern Stephens is at third, Johnny Pesky at short, Bob Doerr at second and Billy Goodman was playing first. On the mound — Ellis Kinder, with Birdie Tebbets behind the plate. And remember, in those days we all wore steel spikes.

Kinder threw me a pitch, right down the middle of the plate, and I really ripped the ball high and long, near the flag pole in center. I swung so hard my spikes got caught in the batters box and I fell down. I quickly looked up to see the ball bounce off the flag pole in center and bounce through DiMaggio's legs. In my haste to get up and run, wouldn't you know, I fell down again. I looked around to see where I was and realized I had now made it to the left-handed batters box — wow, that's progress! Zarilla came over and fielded the ball as I got up and took off with a burst of speed — a flash of light as it were. As crazy as it sounds, the ball slipped out of Zarilla's hand as he was picking it up, and we're just getting started folks! Williams, having run over from center, now picked the ball up. I was almost half way to first and now looking to see what Williams did with the ball. He threw it to the cut-off man, Bobby Doerr. Can you believe, Doerr missed it. I did a double-take and fell down again. I am now only a bit over half way to first, three outfielders have tried to handle the ball, and the relay man has missed it.

Well, at this point Pesky had to go get the ball, and that left second base wide open. I thought, if I took off quickly, I could stretch this thing into a double — I had already lost all hope for a triple. Billy Goodman, though, was a very smart first baseman, and went to cover second. "Thank goodness, that may leave first open," I thought. That was not to be as Birdie Tebbetts, the catcher, had hustled over to cover first. Pesky got the ball and threw to first. Unfortunately, for the Red Sox, pitcher Ellis Kinder had moved in that direction as well, and Pesky's throw hit the pitcher in the shoulder. I was up and off for first again just as I saw the ball hit the pitcher. Bad luck for me, though, because just as I got up, I fell again.

Now, I have been down, count them, four times, three outfielders have handled the ball, the relay man missed a throw, the shortstop recovered the ball, threw and hit the pitcher with it. Well, when the ball hit the pitcher, it bounced over to towards third where Vern Stephens was playing. He surely never figured to be in the play the way it was progressing. By this time I had managed to drag myself close — so close, in fact, that it seemed quicker to finish crawling rather than get up. I completed my crawl to first base. Stephens now with the ball, threw it to Tebbetts covering first, just about the time I reached and touched the bag with my right hand. Then I heard the umpire say,

"Safe!" I had just beaten the throw. Believe it or not, I got a 35,000-fan laughing ovation. I guess you could say I am the proud owner of the longest single on record in the history of baseball. I hit it a long way, and it took a long time to play out — I'll never forget that one!

Team Training
Just a story or two about train travel

For my entire minor league experience, and 6 years into my major league career, we traveled by train. It would be well into the 1950's before an airline would take the ballclub to another city.

In the American League, the eastern teams included Boston, New York, Philadelphia and Washington. The western clubs were Detroit, Chicago, Cleveland and St. Louis. The longest trip I had to make when I was with the White Sox in Chicago was the eastern swing. We would leave Chicago for St. Louis by train. Now comes the tough part. We would end the series on Sunday in St. Louis, board the train and leave around 9:00 PM. We would then travel straight through to Boston, arriving mid-day on Tuesday and play that night. Now that was a trip! These train trips were long and the players would all be together for extended periods of time. Card playing was certainly a favorite past-time among many of my teammates. They would also come up with other types of games to pass the time. Unfortunately, I wasn't very good at most games, but I guess that may be deemed a good thing looking back. Many times during the games, the competition became fierce and they would get angry at one another. Sometimes bad enough that the game would end in a fight. I could live without that.

I remember one incident in particular. After a few beers, Allie Clark and Ferris Fain got into it. I don't remember what caused the problem, but it seems Clark was trying to push Fain through one of the toilet bowls. If memory serves, Ferris didn't fit through it all that well. Well, we would always break-up the fun before someone got hurt. We had a game to play the following day and there was a stunt man that traveled with us to Cleveland. Jackie Price was his name. Jackie had performed many unique stunts on the baseball field. One of his wild stunts was hanging upside down on a moving Jeep and catching fly balls. But one of his greatest stunts was performed on that train. This was during spring training, and we were traveling from Tucson back to the east coast. He kept a black snake in his traveling bag. The snake was about five feet long. One day in the dining car he let the snake loose, and you can imagine the uproar it created. It's not everyday on a train that a snake goes slithering past you. When all the commotion had passed and Price had corralled his snake and headed back to his compartment, I am told, the real excitement took place. It seems the conductor came to our car, and the first guy he talked to was Ken Keltner. Ken was asked to point out the guy with the snake. Not wanting to pass up a chance for a good laugh, Keltner turned and pointed to the black-haired gentleman sitting three rows back. The guy he pointed to was the Cleveland skipper, Lou Boudreau. That was quick thinking. What happened next? Unfortunately for Price, the train was stopped and he and his belongings, including the snake, were dropped off in the desert, near some small town. Life on the road can sure be interesting at times, to say the least.

We also had one of the funniest men in baseball with us in Cleveland — Max Patkin, pictured on the previous page. In one exhibition game, Pat Seerey hit a home run, and as he headed for second base the crowd was really cheering. Pat thought the roar was for him, but, unknown to him, Patkin was following him around the bases. Patkin ended the home run trot with an impressive head first slide into home plate. Needless to say, Pat wanted to choke his eye balls out. Max was one funny fellow, though!

Entertainment in the Dugout
A dugout education

Some of the things players would do in the dugout you were likely to see nowhere else. Gabby Stewart always chewed tobacco. He would lean way back on the dugout bench and when he got his mouth full and was ready to spit, he would aim at his toes. He'd hit them square, and the rest of the gob would just trickle all the way up to his neck. He would always need a clean uniform by the 5th inning. We had a lot of chewers in my day. I, for one, didn't chew. The stuff wound up all over the place, and it was hard to get around at times. You had to watch where you stepped, and especially where you sat. But make no mistake — chewing for many was part of the game, just as much as a bat or ball. And many liked their tobacco.

Harvey Kuenn of Detroit didn't spit as much as Gabby, as he would mix his Beechnut chew with bubble gum. We used to help him get his chew out of the jaw. Unfortunately, chewing cost Harvey his legs, and later his life.

Nellie Fox, another one of my favorite players, always had a chew. Man, would he let the juice fly. Eddie Robinson carried quite a jaw-full too. I saw him one day bragging about the size of his chew. He would take the chew out and put a baseball in his mouth! The only person I knew that could do that was the old comedian Joe E. Brown.

Jimmy Piersall of the Boston Red Sox used to come into our dugout and grab my bat from the rack, telling me if I let him use it he would get me in the Hall of Fame. Guess Jimmy still owes me on that one.

My dugout thoughts wouldn't be complete without touching on a few umpires and managers. They were always at each other. I recall a game when a decision went against Jimmie Dykes. Now, Jimmie could argue and spit at the same time. He could do this with the best of them. On this particular day, Dykes got into it with the third base umpire. Jimmie did all the talking and spitting for about 3 minutes. After that, he ran out of things to say. The umpire who had been waiting patiently for his turn asked, "Are you through?" Dykes barked "Yeah!" The umpire then calmly said, "Jimmie, I missed the play." What a hoot that was.

I know most of you have seen the antics of Billy Martin while managing the Yankees or various other clubs. Martin liked to curse and use bad language in general. He could rattle 'em off with the best of them. But if the fans could hear all the goings on in the dugout, the game would have a little more interest and a lot more entertainment value. In the dugout it wasn't just Martin popping off — everybody took part in the foul language festivities. You would always have dugout cheerleaders and pop-offs — bench jockeys, if you like. Brilliant terms like "Hey, fat-head" or "You flat-footed so-and-so," are just a couple mild-mannered terms that would fly. I can't quote much of the real jockeying that took place as we want the kids to be able to enjoy this book. Today you have the rally caps, and maybe even the old hot foot from time to time.

FAN-tastic

It wouldn't be baseball without the fans

As I recall, both the fans and players of the 1940's through 1960's were not like the fans and players from 1970's and on. When I entered the field of play for the game, I always took a look at the fans in all parks of my era. The seating for the fans were very close to the field of play, much more so than today. I usually felt like the fans were there to see big league players play ball. They got a real enjoyment from the game. Not to say that every now and then you wouldn't have a run in with an opposing fan. That certainly did happen once in a while.

I recall a day we were in Boston. It was late in a tightly contested game. There was a high foul ball hit down the left field line. I raced over, tracking the ball near the left field bleachers. Wouldn't you know, just before making the catch I received a good straight punch from a Boston fan. He caught me square in the nose. At that point I forgot about the ball, grabbed the fan by the right arm and tried to pull him on the field. It was a hot day and he was covered with sweat, so I failed. The batter, however, was called out due to fan interference, and the fan was escorted out of the stadium.

I remember a day in Chicago when I was still playing with the White Sox. I went back to the left field fence to handle a fly ball. Just as I was about to catch the ball, a fan stuck about six squashed beer cups in my glove. Needless to say, I missed the ball, but, again, the batter was called out and the fan was given an early exit from the game.

Then, there was a game in Philadelphia when I was playing for the A's. It was a Sunday afternoon and I was warming up near the dugout as the fans filed in for the game. As I glanced over at the crowd, I noticed a well dressed couple with their two children, perhaps 10 or 11 years old. The kids were also nicely dressed like they may have just come from church. They had seats in the front row — I could reach out and touch them. It was a very warm day so they removed their warm garments, got their refreshments, and proceeded to give me a complete blasting! I was shocked and irritated. They got on me like you wouldn't believe, yelling, "Ya bum, slow footed, lousy player," as well as a few other choice words. No obscenities, but man were they rough. Well, I guess they paid for their seats and they were going to get their money's worth at my expense!

One night in Connie Mack Stadium I had a scare — and I am not easily frightened. There was a group down in the left field bleacher section and they worked me over pretty good all evening. Late in the game, I drifted over near their section and issued a challenge to them — meet me after the game. Between the time of my bold challenge and the time I dressed and left the locker room, I had totally forgotten about my offer. To make things more interesting, I was the last one to leave the clubhouse on this night. As I walked out towards the gate, there was not a teammate to be found. I noticed a car parked close by the gate with six big guys patiently waiting. There was a night watchman nearby, but he was about 80 years old. I can remember thinking, "Boy, this is it!" The first thing I noticed was that the car was a two door and no one was getting out. I walked behind the car, looking for the passenger door to open. That never happened. The car windows were down and then I heard them all saying,

"We stuck around, Gus, to let you know, we think you're a good sport." Then they drove off. It took me about three strides to get to my car and hit the road that evening.

Though our attendance didn't set the world on fire in Philadelphia, we sure had some true blue, loyal fans. Many years later, the Philadelphia Athletics Historical Society was formed. It's a fine organization that has really allowed many players like myself to see the real Philadelphia Athletics fans.

You're Out

Umpires can be your friend

The umpires in baseball seem to often be a topic of interest among baseball players and fans alike. In the 1940's and 1950's, as I remember, the umpires were pretty good. I remember the likes of Art Passarella, Bill Summers, Larry Knapp, Hank Soar, pictured above, and many more. In my 11 years in the major leagues and numerous exhibition games, I never found enough fault with an umpire's decision to get tossed from a game — though I did get tossed once with an ulterior motive — more on that in a minute. Now, I am not saying they did not miss a play or two, but for the most part they got it right.

When they missed a play, or so the manager or a coach thought, everybody heard about it. A couple of the managers that come to mind that were real tough on the umpires were Jimmie Dykes and Earl Weaver (who came along a little later on).

For the most part, in my day the managers were pretty good and respectful, though. Casey Stengel, when he was managing in New York, certainly had his fair share of moments and could be rather entertaining, but no one could put on a show like my long time skipper, Jimmie Dykes. When Dykes would lose it, he would stomp and spit, though I don't think he did this intentionally. It must have been kind of a natural reaction for Jimmie. At times, he was certainly entertainment beyond the cost of a ticket for the fans at the ballpark. It was pretty entertaining to the players as well.

I recall a day when I thought I was going to be tossed, but fortunately was not. We were playing in Boston, and many times the wind would be very strong, blowing out towards center field. I fouled back a ball, over the crowd behind home plate. Boston catcher Del Wilber, along with the Umpire Hank Soar, went back to the stands. I was standing at home plate thinking a play could not be made on the ball. Well, the wind got a hold of the ball and was blowing it back towards the field of play and very close to being in fair territory. I'm still standing at home plate as Wilber is reaching for the ball — he was still in foul territory. He missed the ball, then it bounced up and hit him while he was in foul territory — that would make it a foul ball. Unfortunately, Umpire Soar didn't see it that way and called it a fair ball. I was tossed out easily at first.

Now comes the real story. Manager Dykes had a rule that if you don't run out pop flies, you will be fined $50. Now, I had a real problem. With no other real choice, I started a discussion with the umpire. I claimed that Wilber was in foul territory when he touched the baseball. Obviously, Soar saw it different. I never said anything to the umpire to get tossed, I was just stalling as long as I could. I figured Dykes was waiting for me in the dugout, and I knew that it would cost me $50. There were no hard feelings between Soar and myself as I returned to the dugout. As I approached Jimmie, I turned to Soar and continued the discussion to pass Dykes without having to talk. I headed straight for the water cooler and Dykes was right behind me. Just then I looked out at Passarella at third and yelled, "That goes for you too!" Passarella yelled back to me, "You're out of here!" I headed for the clubhouse. We must have won the game that day because Dykes never approached me with a fine. The next day while we were warming up, Passarella came to me and said, " I saved you fifty bucks last night. I knew Dykes was after you, so I tossed you out." He continued, "Oh — and one other thing. I didn't turn you in to the league, either." That's as close as I ever came to getting tossed, and I don't count that one. The umpires of my day were okay by me.

From observing umpires of today, it seems they are quicker to toss players than in my day. When I played, the umpires seemed to have thicker skin. By that I mean they would listen more to what you had to say. They would give you the chance to get a word in about the play. I see times in today's game when a player looks like he wants to say something, but the umpire is ready to throw him out before the first word is spoken. In fact, I have seen umpires of today invite players into an argument, and that is wrong. I have always thought that the umpires should be the problem solvers with level heads, not problem starters.

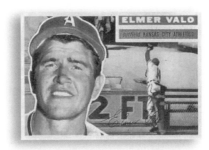

The Rookie

Right field can be right tough

This is just a story, and not a true one, mind you. It's one I like to tell, that brings a smile to me, as well as a good old friend of mine.

This story begins in Philadelphia. The organization brought up a rookie outfielder by the name of Bill Gorman. He was a powerful right-handed hitter with great speed. We were playing a doubleheader against the Boston Red Sox. Elmer Valo was playing right field. In our 6-5 opening game victory, Elmer delivered the game-winning hit.

For the second game, our manager said to Elmer, "Why don't you sit out this one and let the rookie play right field." With a big smile, the veteran said, "Okay Skip." Elmer made himself comfortable with a spot on the bench to enjoy the second game as a spectator.

To start the ballgame, the leadoff batter for Boston hit a towering fly ball to right field. The rookie Gorman patted his glove as he was waiting to make the catch. Unfortunately, it hit the heel of his glove and fell to the ground. Though the manager was disappointed, he figured the rookie didn't have much time to warm up and wasn't too concerned. The next batter hit a ground ball, again to right, for a base hit. This time Gorman let the ball roll between his legs — his second error of the inning. Now there are runners on second and third. The next batter hit a line drive single — you guessed it, to Gorman in right again. He ranged far to his right to make the stop, but in his haste to throw home he threw it over the dugout for yet another error. By this time the manager was visibly upset and on the top step of the dugout yelling for time. He turned to his veteran Valo and said, "Take right field — this rookie is driving me nuts!"

With a big smile on his face and all the confidence of a veteran, Valo took over in right. The manager could settle down with his veteran in right — now he could breath more easily. Or so he thought. As fate would have it, Valo dropped a fly ball for an error and then let a ball go between his legs. Before the inning was over, 7 runs had scored on 5 errors before the A's would even come to bat.

When Elmer came off the field, the manager met him at the foul line to find out what was going on in right field. Being a quick-thinking veteran has its advantages. Elmer had the perfect answer on the spot, "That rookie has got right field so screwed up, nobody could play it."

Now I am sure many of you are asking, "Who is Bill Gorman?" Well, Bill happens to be one of my best friends. His background is long and covers over 30 years as a general manager of minor league baseball clubs, most of them at the Triple-A level. He joined the Fresno Grizzlies of the Pacific Coast League in 2001 and remained general manager through the 2004 season when he was fired by the incoming administration, led by Rick Roush and Company. Bill Gorman is now working outside baseball, but should be back some time soon in my estimation. He sure loved this story when I told it to him.

A Final Diamond Gem or Two
Baseball life is really a blast

A book could be filled with stories of the true legends of baseball that I was fortunate enough to play with and against — here's a small sampling.

I begin with Luke Appling, pictured above, of the Chicago White Sox, or "Old Aches and Pains," as some folks called him. A Hall of Fame player, Luke played 20 years with the Sox and was a lifetime .300 hitter that could foul off pitch, after pitch, until he got the one he wanted. Allie Reynolds of the Yankees once walked him intentionally after he fouled off several pitches. On this day in Boston, the Red Sox bench was really riding Luke. I followed him in the batting order. During his at-bat he stepped out of the box and asked me, "Who's doing the yelling?" I pointed to one of the bench jockeys, and on the next pitch he lined one into the dugout — now that's bat control!

In the same series in Boston, Luke asked me to join him and Red Sox pitcher Ellis Kinder for dinner. Upon arrival I noticed that dinner had turned into a liquid diet only. It was a Saturday night and I thought, "What the heck can it hurt?" So I had a couple beers with the guys, but they were really tossing them back. In all honesty — I couldn't keep up. These two guys were nearing 40, and I was a young, wide-eyed rookie. I told Luke we better go. After all, we had a doubleheader the next day, which was Sunday. We walked out of the club and the sun was coming up! I couldn't believe it. We grabbed a bite to eat and headed for the ballpark.

That day we opted out of batting practice and stayed very clear of the manager. Now, Luke and Ellis were pretty soused, and I didn't feel too good myself. I sure found out one thing, though — I couldn't do what they did. The game starts and who do you think is on the mound for the Red Sox? You guessed it — Ellis Kinder. Kinder walks the first two, then Luke was hitting third. He drops a short line drive into right and the bases are loaded. Now it's my turn. As I am ambling up to the plate, time is called and there is a meeting on the mound. A few minutes pass and the public address announces that Kinder will have to leave the game due to food poisoning. Everyone on the field knew what was wrong, but obviously the fans didn't. Ellis was sick, but it sure wasn't what he had eaten. As Ellis departed a hard throwing right-hander by the name of Willard Nixon came on in relief. The very first pitch he threw to me was a fast ball. I tagged it for a bases-loaded dinger, though I am not sure how I pulled that one off.

Here is the story about Luke. Bombed as he was, he went 3-for-4 in each game and never missed a beat. Can you believe that? I, on the other hand, was not heard from again, after my first time at-bat. For that twin-bill, you could stick a fork in me — I was done. And good ole Ellis was long gone — even before me. After that experience, I didn't make too many dinners or nights on the town with Luke. As a matter of fact, he didn't pull too many more all-nighters like the one in Boston. He was an amazing athlete and competitor, though. At 42 years of age, he hit .301 in 1949. He even played some first base, when Chico Carrasquel came along to play shortstop. It was a pleasure to play with Luke Appling — I learned a lot from him. The guy was a real Hall of Famer in my book.

Floyd Baker was our third baseman in 1949 with Chicago. Now, Floyd

was a fine player and a key member of the St. Louis Browns 1944 pennant winning team — the only Brownie team to ever win a pennant. To round out the infield we had Appling at short, Cass Michaels at second and Steve Souchock at first. Now, no one could field their position better than Baker. He had a good year in 1949, though he hit only .260 for the season. In the spring of 1950 I met up with Floyd Baker and Luke Appling in Chicago. We figured we could get our contracts settled and signed, and do a little public relations work, as well.

The contract negotiations were to be with our general manager, Frank Lane. Many referred to him as "Trader Frank," (if the shoe fits, wear it, I guess.) Well, I was having trouble with Lane, and so was Floyd. Luke had signed earlier with no problem at all. Baker wanted a raise, and Frank simply wouldn't agree to what he was asking for. After much negotiating, Lane said to Floyd, "You didn't hit .300 last year." Baker's reply was short and sweet to the general manager, "Nobody hit 300 through me, either." I guess his answer worked to a degree because he got a small raise. Ironically, Floyd would hit well over .300 for the 1950 edition of the White Sox.

I never signed with Mr. Lane that year. Chuck Comisky, now the president of the club, came by and asked me what the hold up was with me signing my new contract. I told him that Mr. Lane and I just couldn't come to terms on a new deal. He saw what the offer was, revised it, and I signed. I believe that negotiation was one reason Frank Lane traded me as soon as he did.

Another incident occurred in 1950. The White Sox had picked up an

BOB LEMON
CLEVELAND INDIANS

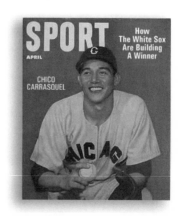

SPORT
APRIL
How The White Sox Are Building A Winner
CHICO CARRASQUEL

outfielder by the name of Marv Rickert. Now, Marv was a pretty fair hitting left-hander, and we were heading for Cleveland and a four game series against the Tribe. Hall of Famer Bob Lemon was the mainstay of that staff and was pitching against us on a Saturday afternoon. First time up, Rickert took three over the plate and didn't offer at one. Next time at the plate ditto — and yet again in his third time up, leaving him with nine pitches in three at-bats, totaling three strikeouts. On the fourth trip to the dish, Cleveland catcher, Jim Hegan, went to the mound to talk to Lemon. They decided on a sinker for the first pitch to Marv on his fourth at-bat. Well, wouldn't you know that he belted it for a home run. When Rickert reaches second he stops and yells, "Lemon, you have to be the dumbest pitcher in the American League — I set a trap for you and you fell right into it." Well, I'm not sure who was trapping who, but we lost as that was our only run for the game.

1950 was the last year for Luke Appling at shortstop as Chico Carrasquel, a Cuban player, was to be our new one. Unfortunately for Chico, he could speak no English. About the middle of the season they found he wasn't eating properly, and the reason was simple — all he could say in English was, "Ham and Eggs." To make life a little easier for Chico, they signed a Cuban pitcher to help him out who could speak English. Seems there was never a dull moment in the bigs for me.

Oh — and how I remember the Chicago White Sox and our general manager Frank Lane. It was a bright, sunny day in Detroit with the breeze blowing to left. Frank always sat behind the dugout and carried every newspaper he could get his hands on. We're trailing 1-0 in the top half of the ninth. I led off with a walk, then Eddie Robinson singled to left. Runners were at first and second with nobody out. Hank Majeski came to the plate and was asked to sacrifice. This really caught everybody off guard. First pitch was a fastball right down the middle of the plate. Hank squared to bunt but missed, and I was thrown out trying to scramble back to second. I got to the dugout, and Frank was red as a beet — man was he mad. On the next pitch the hit and run sign was given to Hank. That also was a surprise with the lack of speed Robbie had at first. Well, Hank missed that pitch, too, and Robbie was out by 20 feet at second. After all the dust settled, Detroit had thrown two pitches, gotten two outs and had two strikes on Majeski. At this point I though Frank might explode — he was boiling mad. Here comes the next pitch — strike three.

Hank struck out. Three pitches, three outs, and we go home losing, 1-0. With that Frank stood up and let fly all of his newspapers. They were all over the field. In addition, he let the whole team have it afterwards. He was one hot-tempered guy. Frank certainly earned his nickname, too — "Trader Lane." He was so trade-happy that he even swapped managers once. While serving as the general manager in Cleveland, he sent Joe Gordon to Detroit for Jimmie Dykes. In 1951 he traded me for Minnie Minoso. When he got the general manager job with the St. Louis Cardinals, the first guy he tried to deal was Stan the Man. I guess that didn't go over so well in the front office, so he did the next best thing — he worked out a deal that sent future Hall of Fame player, Red Schoendienst, to Milwaukee.

I don't mind saying that I didn't care much for Frank Lane at first, but I did grow to admire and respect him. I even heard later on that after he traded me to Philadelphia he tried to get me back. When the Athletics would play in Chicago, Frank would always sit in the upper deck. Dave Philley and I were both former White Sox players under Mr. Lane that he traded. Seems to me we hit very well against the White Sox — maybe we had a little extra incentive. Every series, Dave and I would joke that Frank might just jump from his upper deck seat.

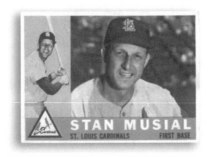

A Teenager at the Ball Park
Meeting George Susce

I added this small story, simply because it amazes me how long a few seconds of interaction can stay in one's memory. Something quite insignicant to one person, can really be memorable for another. Add to that the small chance of ever crossing paths again, at a professional level, and you have a truly unique story. I think this is one of those stories.

In my hometown of Beaumont, Texas, when I was 16 years old, I went to see the Beaumont Exporters play. Beaumont was the farm team for the Detroit Tigers. I think the visiting team was Galveston. As kids, we always went out early to try to get a ball. In batting practice the players would often hit balls over the fence. I was unlucky on this day and didn't get one. When the game started I would sit in the bleachers and hope to retrieve a foul ball.

By the 7th inning I was still shutout, so I made a visit to the short fence near the visiting team's bullpen. George Susce was the bullpen coach, and being a catcher back when he played minor league baseball, he would often warm up the relief pitchers. As a young kid I followed the game closely and knew all the players — so I knew who George Susce was. He was sitting on the ground and his catcher's mitt was next to him holding 3 brand new balls. I remember very well saying, "Mr. Susce, can I have one of those balls?" His reply, "Go sit down, son, I have work to do and I can't give you a ball." I was disappointed, but I understood.

Years later when I was drafted by the Cleveland Indians, I went to spring training in Tucson, Arizona. The first thing I looked at was the team roster. I was amazed at some of the names, but I also noted that one of the coaches under manager Lou Boudreau was none other than George Susce. Being a young man that would speak up, it didn't take long for me to introduce myself and relate the story of my minor league experience. Of course, he didn't recall the incident, but I think it had something to do with our relationship over the years. I want to say at this time that Mr. Susce was a fine man and a good coach.

I didn't see George again until 1955, when the Philadelphia Athletics moved to Kansas City and George was again a coach, under Lou Boudreau.

George was a very quiet man and hardly talked to any one except his bullpen pitchers. It was 1955 or 1956 and his son, George, Jr., made the pitching staff with the Boston Red Sox. On a trip to Kansas City, the young Red Sox pitcher George Susce, Jr., was on the mound and I tagged him for a game winning home run. George was really silent toward me on the bench. I am sure he would have liked his son to have struck me out. I don't remember what happened to George, when Boudreau was fired, but I think he went on for many more years in baseball.

I'm sure you recognize the fine gentleman on the opposite page — Connie Mack. He was a true man of the game.

MY ALL-STARS

The Tall Tactician

My time with Connie Mack

One of the truly great legends of the game is Connie Mack. When I first came to Chicago in 1949, Mr. Mack came to my attention. I knew what a tremendous baseball background he had. The record stands for itself, as well as the championship seasons he had in Philadelphia. He managed some of the all-time greats of the game. Players the likes of Jimmie Foxx, Al Simmons, Robert "Lefty" Grove, Jimmie Dykes, Mickey Cochrane and Eddie Collins are just a few — you could go on and on.

One memory I have takes me back to a day in Chicago against the Athletics. Lou Brissie was pitching that day, and I had read where Mr. Mack, on many occasions, called the pitches himself. When I came to bat I saw Brissie looking into the dugout, so I did the same thing. I saw Mr. Mack, with a twist of the wrist, calling for a curve ball. Then it was Lou and I, eye-balling each other. He fired the curve, just as Mr. Mack had called for. I knew what was coming, and though I don't remember what took place, I do know I had one good cut at that pitch. I talked about this with Lou later but he didn't recall it — I can tell you I sure did, though.

1950 was the last year for Mr. Mack as a manager. After 50 years he was stepping down. He turned the managerial duties over to his long-time favorite player, Jimmie Dykes. Dykes had been a hard-nosed player on many of Mr. Mack's teams of the 1920's. I was traded to the Athletics in the early part of the 1951 campaign. It was there I met Connie Mack, the A's owner. He was a very distinguished person with great character. I very seldom saw Mr. Mack at Connie Mack Stadium (before the stadium was named for him, it was called Shibe Park), but I would often see him on our road trips and in spring training.

I remember him sitting in the hotel lobby one day in Cleveland, and I walked by and stood before this great baseball legend and said, "Hello." I recall the great feeling I had when he looked at me for some time and said, "I know you — you're number 19." Mr. Mack had reached the age where names escaped him at times, though that was not always the case. I recall another day in spring training at West Palm Beach, Florida. We were playing an exhibition game and I had rushed to the club house to change shirts as the game was

Here you can see Mr. Mack having some fun with fellow Hall of Famer, Chief Bender.

about to start. As I was running out the door, Mr. Mack was coming in. I nearly ran over him, making one of the most graceful dancing moves ever seen to avoid a collision. To this day I recall, so very well, what he said to me, "Have a good game, Gus." That was the only time, I can remember him calling me by name.

Mr. Mack often mispronounced names. I heard from other players that when playing the Yankees he would refer to the Yankee centerfielder, "Dom-a-gio." Of course he meant DiMaggio. The shortstop was "Riz-a-to" — you get the idea. I don't recall him ever trying my name of Zernial.

I guess all managers have their methods of tracking players and, like any good one, so did Mr. Mack. Curfews existed on all ballclubs, usually put in play by the manager. At times it seemed it was the player's job to find ways to break curfews without detection while the manager specialized in apprehension. When Mr. Mack was managing it was said he would station himself in the lobby at midnight so he could monitor who got on the elevator after the curfew. He must have taught Dykes a trick or two. Jimmie would give the elevator operator a baseball and ask him to have it signed by all players that came in after curfew. Some guys never caught on.

I'd like to pass on a thank you to the Philadelphia Athletics Historical Society. Because of their events I have been fortunate enough to meet many of Connie Mack's family — the McGillicuddy family. That was a special treat for me having played for Mr. Mack in Philadelphia.

The Greatest Hitter I Ever Saw

Ted Williams had no equal with the lumber

During my 11 years in major league baseball, the best hitter I ever saw was the Splendid Splinter, Ted Williams. Many fans and opposing players would come to the park early just to see Teddy Ballgame take his swings at batting practice. The rhythm of his swing and the power he generated were amazing to watch. When the game got under way, you sure hoped he didn't look so good.

He hit with such authority that his fielding and base running were often overlooked. I saw him play the Green Monster Wall at Fenway as good as anyone, and he always knew when to take the extra base. From time-to-time as a promotion, Ted and I would have a home run hitting contest before a ball game in Philadelphia. Although home run hitting contests are done much differently today, it was the same general theme. You got batting practice fastballs and just tried to launch 'em — hit 'em as far as you could. I think we held three of these contests and I won once.

Ted was a student of the game. He would study the opposing pitcher like no other player did. And you can bet the pitchers knew it. He was the best at waiting for his pitch in his zone that he could drive. The best I've seen today is Barry Bonds of the San Francisco Giants.

This "student of the game" approach is one of the things that made Ted great. Obviously, his great ability, attitude and application to the game helped an awful lot, too. In 1951, I had the opportunity to battle Ted during one of his best seasons in the game. I led the league in home runs with 33. In that same year, Ted led or was in the top 10 in nearly every batting category. Amazingly, he did this almost every year he played. It was a pleasure to have played against him.

In that great baseball year of 1941, when he and Joe DiMaggio were wrecking American League pitching, I believe they should have awarded two MVP trophies. Joe had that 56-game hitting streak while Ted hit .406. Joe hit well over .300 for that season as well. Neither of these two numbers have been surpassed, in all of the seasons of baseball played since then. In fact, they have rarely been challenged by the players who've played after them.

I had the opportunity to play 3 seasons against Joe, and I played my entire career against Ted. There could not be two players more opposite than these two. They ran differently, fielded differently, acted differently — heck, they even batted differently as Ted hit left-handed and Joe right. They did, however, have at least one thing in common — they each had three letters in their first name and eight letters in their last name. Just figured I'd toss in that little piece of trivia.

In 1951, Ted Williams won the American League Babe Ruth Award. I received some information on the criteria used to choose the winner, and was really proud to see how my '51 season stacked up against Teddy Ballgame's. On the following page, I have complied a small sampling of a few categories, and names that were used to determine the award winner.

Ted and Joe smile for the camera before a game.

Here is Ted inspecting his bat — nobody understood the art of hitting better than he did.

A few of the 1951
Babe Ruth award categories

Home Runs
1. Gus Zernial 33
2. Ted Williams 30
3. Eddie Robinson 29

Slugging
1. Ted Williams .556
2. Larry Doby .512
3. Gus Zernial .511

Home Run %
1. Gus Zernial 5.78
2. Ted Williams 5.65
3. Luke Easter 5.56

Extra Base Hits
1. Gus Zernial 68
2. Ted Williams 62
3. Minnie Minoso 58

Runs Batted In
1. Gus Zernial 129
2. Ted Williams 126
3. Eddie Robinson 117

Isolated Power
1. Gus Zernial .243
2. Ted Williams .237
3. Vic Wertz .226

Ozark Ike's All-Stars
Diamond talent of the 1940's & 1950's

One of the things I have always wanted to do is list, in my estimation, the best players I competed against and played with during my playing days. Down through the years, I have seen many "All-Time Great" teams selected for many different types of sports. They are chosen in a variety of ways, ranging from fan selection to press balloting and all points in between. Here are all the guys who made my club for the record:

First Base — Ferris Fain, Mickey Vernon & Eddie Robinson
Second Base — Nelson Fox, Bobby Doerr & Billy Martin

Third Base — George Kell, Al Rosen & Brooks Robinson

Shortstop — Luke Appling, Luis Aparicio & Phil Rizzuto

Catcher — Yogi Berra, Jim Hegan & Joe Astroth

Left Field — Ted Williams, Gene Woodling & Roy Sievers

Center Field — Mickey Mantle, Joe DiMaggio, Larry Doby & Dave Philley

Right Field — Al Kaline, Hank Bauer & Elmer Valo

Left-Handed Pitcher — Whitey Ford, Bobby Shantz, Billy Pierce, Mel Parnell & Herb Score

Right-Handed Pitcher — Bob Lemon, Bob Feller, Jim Bunning, Early Wynn, Bob Turley & Allie Reynolds

To the best of my memory, this is the order that I would place them in by position. As you will read, I sure had a tough time choosing an order for some of these positions — these guys are all tops in my book.

In the infield I'll go with Ferris Fain at first. He was just about as good with the leather as there was in the business. To top that off, he led the league league in hitting two years in a row. Vernon is close, but I chose Fain because of his fielding. Eddie Robinson was the power guy in this group. Nelson Fox at second was a self-made player — he was a good hitter and turned the double-play as good as anyone I've ever seen. He was a tough guy to strike out, too. Doerr and Martin were just a shade behind him. At third, I have two Hall of Fame players. I went with Kell because I played against him more often and saw him on a regular basis. I have to say, though, it is tough to go against Robinson. Probably should be a tie. The power of Rosen was uncanny — he led the league twice in homers. Maybe a three-way tie? At shortstop, it has to be Appling as he played 20 years for the White Sox and earned a spot in the Baseball Hall of Fame, boasting a lifetime .310 batting average. I picked him over two real good ones, though, in Rizzuto and Aparicio — all three could field and hit.

The outfield was no easy task, either. In left field, though, without a doubt, it's Ted Williams. He was the best hitter in baseball during my time and possibly of all-time. Ted was not a bad outfielder, and he could always beat you with just one swing of the bat. Gene Woodling and Roy Sievers were both very steady ballplayers. Roy could really swing the bat, and had great power. I really don't have to say much about center field — Mantle, DiMaggio and

He's not only an All-Star catcher to me, but a pretty good interview too! That's me with Yogi a few years after we left the game. I always enjoyed chatting with him and it seems we always had a laugh or two.

Doby, all three Hall of Fame players. I feel honored to have played against them all. Mantle once told a group of us that had he taken care of himself, he could have hit 800 home runs — and of that I have no doubt. DiMaggio was named player of the century, and there was none better. Larry Doby was the first black player in the American League. He was a very steady hitter with good power, and a fine fielder as well. Al Kaline stood above all his peers as a right fielder. A Hall of Fame member, he also enjoys membership in the 3,000 Hit Club (a pretty exclusive group). Hank Bauer was such a solid player and a productive part of so many Yankee World Series victories. I especially remember Bauer as having a very good arm. To round it out, I have a steady outfielder for our Philadelphia ball clubs — Elmer Valo. When you talk about a reliable player with superb longevity, your talking about Valo.

Mound Masters
Some thoughts on my All-Star pitchers

When it comes to an all-time pitchers list, I believe it could be much longer than the names I have here. My list is based only on the pitchers I faced during my career. In my estimation, though, no names would come before any of these guys. This group could really get it done on the mound.

Whitey Ford would be number one on my list, a consistent winner. He had all the pitches, too. You had to bear down on each and every pitch he threw. He was very tough to hit, using a good fastball to set up his breaking ball which was equally effective. Whitey was a consistent 20-game winner and still has the record for consecutive scoreless innings in World Series play. I guess you could say that I'm one of those, playing against him, that helped put him in the Hall of Fame.

My former teammate, Bobby Shantz, makes my list. There was no pitcher who could field their position better than Bobby. He had back-to-back Hall of Fame years. In 1951 he won 18 games for the Philadelphia Athletics, and followed that campaign in 1952 with a 24-game winning season. That season he pitched great in the All-Star game and won the American League MVP. Late in the season he was hit in the left wrist by a fast ball from Walt Masterson and never seemed to recover. My thought is that if he had stayed

That's me with Al Rosen, one of my All-Star third basemen. Al could field and hit with the best of them.

healthy, he would have a plaque in Cooperstown today. The stories of his fielding abilities are still talked about.

Billy Pierce of the Chicago White Sox and Mel Parnell of the Boston Red Sox were two very consistent winners. They may have fallen short of the Hall of Fame, that just may be because the electing members never had to face them. Nonetheless, they sure make it in my book.

When it comes to right-handers, I faced many good ones, but Bob Lemon would be first up for me. Bob, a Hall of Fame member, won 20 or more games 7 years in a row — that's tough to do! And I'm not the only one who thinks Bob could really bring it. Ted Williams always said Lemon was one of the best he ever saw — that's enough for me. It took me some time, but I learned to hit Lemon in my last few years. I got a tip from a Hall of Fame player by the name of Al Simmons of Philadelphia A's fame. At the time I got the tip, I told Simmons I had already put Lemon in the Hall of Fame.

I faced Bob Feller many times before he retired. In all honesty, I could go on and on about his fastball and curve, but with 3 no-hitters and 12 one-hitters — need I say anything more? Simple fact was you had to be extremely alert when facing "Rapid Robert." I was watching a minor league game with Bob one day and the pitcher was clocked at 94 miles per hour. Bob smiled and said, "If that guy is throwing 94, I must have thrown 110." And you know what —I believe him and I'm not the only one who does. He flat-out threw hard, and I mean HARD! Pitchers were not clocked in our day, though. The radar guns they use readily today weren't around yet.

Some other pitchers who sure would get a vote from me are Early Wynn and his 300 victories and Jim Bunning, perhaps a better pitcher than a Senator (though I guess he does all right). Jim tossed 2 no-hitters, one in each league. One of his no-hit performances was a perfect game. I was in the outfield for Detroit when he no-hit Boston at Fenway Park. And last, but not least, was flame-thrower Bob Turley of the Yankees — he could just flat out throw smoke.

This is the form that won, Bobby Shantz, the 1952 American League MVP award. I am proud to call him my teammate and good friend.

It's Outta Here

The American League's top home run hitters of the '50s

The top five American League sluggers in the decade of the '50s each blasted more than 200 home runs. The members of this elite club include Yogi Berra and Mickey Mantle of the New York Yankees, yours truly, Gus Zernial, of the Chicago White Sox and Philadelphia Athletics, Ted Williams of the Boston Red Sox and Larry Doby of the Cleveland Indians.

Now, I am not a big numbers person, and in all honesty, had not figured my home run numbers, and how they fit into history of the 1950's. A few years back, though, this particular statistical breakdown (of 200 home runs hit during that decade) was brought to my attention. I'm really proud to be member of this 1950's home run club. The Yankees boasted the one-two punch of Berra's 256 long balls, followed by Mantle's 252. I checked in with 232 homers, followed by Williams with 227 and Doby with 217, to round out the top five. Mixed in with my 232 home runs were 9 grand slams and a league leading 33 homers in 1951. Of the 33 homers, 22 were hit with men on base.

While I was with the White Sox I set a new club record with 29 home runs in 1950. I also tied the American League mark with 4 home runs in a doubleheader. With the Philadelphia Athletics I tied a record by belting 6 home runs in 3 consecutive games. The next day I hit another, for 7 homers in 4 consecutive games, to tie another American League record. Ralph Kiner of the Pirates holds the major league record with 8 homers in 4 games.

Mickey Mantle was the most dynamic power-hitter of the decade in my estimation. He had a season high of 56 home runs in 1956. Possessing amazing power from both sides of the plate, he was the Triple Crown winner in that same year.

Here's another fun fact — all of the above mentioned long ball hitters were elected to the Baseball Hall of Fame except your's truly. I'd say I'm keeping pretty good company these days. Nonetheless, I was chosen as a member of the Connie Mack All-Century Team by the Philadelphia Athletics Historical Society. I share outfield duties with Al Simmons and Sam Chapman — not bad company again. To be named, along side those talented players, is truly an honor for me.

This is the press photo after I had blasted 6 home runs over 3 consceutive games. I would go on the add one more in my next game to finish with 7 homers over a 4 game stretch. Many of you will recognize this as the picture used for my 1952 Topps baseball card.

2007 All-Star Game

Recognizing the game's greatest players

In 1953, I played in the All-Star Game at Crosley Field, in Cincinnati, Ohio. The National League defeated the American League, 5-1. I remember facing Robin Roberts and Warren Spahn. I singled off Roberts, but was K'd by the great left-hander, Spahn. That game was truly a highlight in my career. The All-Star games played during the 1940's and 1950's were like a sandlot pickup game, though, compared to today's game.

I just watched the All-Star game played in San Francisco. The game was won by the American League, 5-4. The fanfare given the game today, and rightly so, is fantastic. I felt my adrenaline flowing during the tribute given to Willie Mays. He looked as though he loved every moment of it, and he should. A few years ago the same kind of tribute was given to Ted Williams. I felt the same way then. I am glad the game has evolved over the years into what it has become today — a great baseball event.

I shared a cab with Warren Spahn to the 1953 All-Star Game. As I recall, I told Warren I would hit one off him if I faced him. Unfortunately for me, that didn't happen — we had a chuckle just the same. The game was packed, as over 30,000 fans flocked to Crosley Field, but there was not the fanfare today's game enjoys. That part, the pageantry, was all to happen later.

I wonder who will be the next player honored? It has to be some one that is still living today. My choice would have to be Stan the Man. Musial fits the category of Williams and Mays, and certainly deserves that type of tribute. In the future we have the likes of Carl Yastrzemski, Reggie Jackson and Cal Ripken, to name just a few that deserve this type of honor. I look at these players with great admiration for how they played the game.

On the opposite page is a comic book cover, featuring the popular Ozark Ike character. That's the same Ozark Ike, I was nicknamed after. I was given this comic by Carl Goldberg of the Philadelphia Athletics Historical Society. Every time I see an Ozark Ike comic, it gets me thinking about baseball.

The Long Ball
Master of the home run

I am both pleased and proud to have hit 237 major league home runs for my career. Leading the league in 1951 with 33 home runs and posting a career high of 42 in 1953 were both real thrills for me. I know from experience just how tough it is to hit a home run. Maybe that's why I respect all the different era home run kings to some degree. This story is about The Sultan of Swat — Babe Ruth. To me and many others, Ruth will always be known as the champ as far as the long ball goes (no pun intended.) This is, of course, to take nothing away from what Hank Aaron has done, or what Barry Bonds is about to do, or, for that matter, any others that follow. It's just the era in which Babe did it that makes him stand alone to me.

In the early 1920's Ruth was hitting more home runs than entire teams combined — that's amazing. In 1927 no player was even close to challenging the 60 homers that Ruth blasted. In my mind he was by far the best at what he did. He would hit over 50 home runs 4 times during his career. At the time that was unheard of. At the end of his career his 714 homers seemed to be completely out of reach.

In the 1950's along came Hank Aaron, a tremendous home run hitter as well. I don't believe he ever hit 50 in one season, but he sure tallied many 40-plus home run seasons. I remember playing against Aaron when he was a thin shortstop coming up in the minors. His feat of passing the Babe will always be remembered, but it's still not like the Babe to me. There is just something about the likes of Lou Gehrig, Hack Wilson, Hank Greenberg, Jimmie Foxx, Mel Ott, Ralph Kiner, Ted Williams, Eddie Mathews and so on. They just seem to hold a different persona for me — perhaps it is because I remember those days so well.

For such a long time you couldn't open a sports page without reading about Barry Bonds, Mark McGwire or Sammy Sosa and the use of steroids in baseball. This issue should have been dealt with long before it was placed front and center by Jose Canseco in his book. Let me add my 2 cents about the use of steroids. Though I don't condone the use of drugs for that purpose, players like the three mentioned here possess tremendous eye-to-hand coordination — a skill that is critical to every power hitter. These drugs don't enhance that skill. I believe if you give a .240 hitter who averages 19 homers a year, all the drugs he can hold, he'll still give you similar production. Nonetheless, I congratulate Bonds, McGwire and Sosa for their home run feats. At the end of the day, however, "The Bambino" will always be the home run king to me.

Learn to Hit
My perspective on hitting a baseball

Hitting a baseball, no matter what league you're in, can't be taught. I believe it has to be learned by the batter. The fundamentals of hitting, however, can be taught. How to develop a proper batting stance, how to hold the bat, how to stride or not stride. The eye-to-hand coordination must be developed by the player himself. Similarly, following the ball and learning your strike zone will come with more batting repetition. I had to learn, just as the players of today have to learn. The top hitters of today have that fantastic, eye-to-hand coordination. Barry Bonds of the Giants, and Jim Edmonds of the Cards are a couple that come to mind for me, but there are too many to name.

It's hard to explain exactly, but let's look at it like this. Take a player of my era and one of today's game. Let's look at Ted Williams of the Boston Red Sox and Bobby Bonds of the San Francisco Giants. These are two of the best at their trade, and here's why. They each study the pitcher they're facing. Believe it or not, these guys have a good understanding of how many curve balls and fast balls the pitcher they are facing will throw. They know approximately how many they will get over the plate, and they pick their hitting zone. This is what many players simply can't learn. Williams and Bonds are patient and wait for a pitch in their zone. When they get it, they hit it, and, more often than not, with power. I believe this is a key reason why you see so few .300 hitters, both in my era and today.

Hitters like Williams and Bonds couldn't help their own teammates with the eye-to-hand coordination — a large degree of that is natural to those guys. You could go back and fourth for hours and never get anywhere. There is only one sure thing, and that is that there are never going to be very many

.300 hitters.

Ted Williams once said to be a .300 hitter, you have to hit the ball on the nose 6 to 7 times out of every 10 times at bat. Remember, if you have a .300 average, you fail 7 out of every 10 plate appearances. Many outfielders and infielders take away base hits with fine fielding plays. Can you imagine how many times Williams hit the ball on the nose to hit .406 in 1941? You can bet your last dollar it must have been a bunch.

Years before Williams was playing there were many more .400 hitters. Batting averages can fool you a bit, though. Many players in the early years tried to make contact with the ball, simply putting it in play somewhere. That resulted in higher batting averages. Typically, the power numbers were lower in those days as a result. Players of today and yesterday have spent many hours talking about hitting. In my estimation, about 75% fail to solve it. Players have spent hours and hours in batting cages practicing, and this repetition can be useful — don't get me wrong. But no batting cage pitching machine can throw a ball like Bob Feller, Bob Lemon, Sandy Koufax, Don Drysdale, Bob Gibson or today's fire-ballers like Randy Johnson and Nolan Ryan to name a few. You must develop other ways to deal with good pitching and it's not always physical but much more mental.

Thousands of players spend hours and hours throwing, fielding and running — thousands can perform those disciplines well. The best way to the big leagues, though, is LEARN TO HIT! How do you do that? Develop your own strike zone, the area you can handle the pitch most consistently, and hit it on the nose. Don't try to hit balls in the pitcher's zone. I have seen good pitchers win a ball game, seldom throwing the pitches over the plate. The batters help them out, offering at balls out of the strike zone. A disciplined hitter has a much better chance of being a successful hitter.

Triple-A Baseball
3-key components to success

My Triple-A baseball consists of these: Ability - Attitude - Application. Many major league players, as well as minor league, college and high school players, can't put these three simple things together at the same time — day in and day out, all season long. There's no doubt to me that this is true of all sports, but let's keep it to baseball for our purposes here.

All good athletes have the ability to play, but there are many different attitudes, ranging from very good to outright bad. We see bad attitudes with far too much regularity. Things such as, "I don't feel good today," or "it was a lousy field," are just a couple of examples. Obviously, it is always easy to just blame the coach when any problem arises. To me, the right attitude is always going to be positive, knowing that you're going to have a good day or hoping you can deliver the winning hit to help your team win. Whether you are playing that day or on the bench, keep a good attitude. Be a good communicator. A player may think he has the good attitude to go along with his ability, but if it is not applied on the field of play, the result, more than likely, will be failure that day. That type of problem can also affect teammates. Assuming the teammates are thinking in a similar fashion, the ballclub is probably doomed to lose.

To be a good team, I believe each player has to put the Triple-A's together at the same time — that makes a winner. There are times when you see a team on the field that does not figure to win regularly during a full season. Somehow, a good manager or coach, though, is able to convince all players to use these fundamentals every day and they become winners — what many call over-achievers. The skipper of the club then wins the "Manager of the Year" award. It all depends on how coachable the players are. What you see today are many high-fives when a player does virtually nothing. It's great to cheer when a player contributes, but to cheer for no apparent reason makes little sense to me.

I have noticed many players going to the plate over the past several years with the attitude that they can't hit this pitcher. The result typically is a poor effort. On the other hand, I have seen just the opposite at work. Some of the best I've witnessed came along many years after I retired. The likes of Boggs, Carew, Jackson, McCovey, Clark and Bonds, just to name a few. These guys applied these principles daily. Didn't other players on their teams learn something from their example? I have said before you can't teach hitting. There is a lot more to hitting than having the right stance at the plate. Watching the flight of the ball, timing, know your own hitting zone, making the pitcher come to you — those are a few things that you learn on your own. Apply your ability with the right attitude and you certainly increase your chance of a positive result.

Who were the players of my day that had the right attitude and applied it properly? Start with the Yankees, Joe D, Yogi Berra, Tommy Henrich and Phil Rizzuto. I could name all the Yankees for that matter. They won the pennant 9 of the 11 years that I faced them. How about Boston? Ted Williams, Johnny Pesky, Bobby Doerr and Dom DiMaggio. From Washington you have Roy Sievers as a stand-out performer, with Eddie Yost. From the Philadelphia Athletics there was Eddie Joost, Ferris Fain and Gus Zernial (I'll put myself in that group). The Detroit Tigers had Al Kaline and Harvey Kuenn. There's Minnie Minoso and many more that I failed to mention. Let's jump to the National League where Duke Snider, Roy Campanella, Willie Mays, Stan the Man, Johnny Mize, Enos Slaughter, Aaron, Mathews and Banks, and again you could go on from there. Many of today's and yesterday's players have, or had, the Triple-A's of baseball — it's one of the reasons that many of the stars of the game achieve what they do.

Scouting Builds Winners
Spanning the globe for baseball talent

Looking back at my baseball career, one of the areas where my knowledge is lacking is scouting. I have not had the opportunity to meet and talk with many scouts during my career. They are, undoubtedly, an extremely valuable part of each team, and for the most part, overlooked and under appreciated.

When one is scouting an opponent, a key element they are looking for is hitting. They want to identify the players who are hot with the bat and how to pitch to them — what are the opposing team's pitchers doing to get these hitters out. Scouts possess a tremendous knowledge of the game and, more importantly, knowledge of the players. What is the scout looking for when they are signing new talent? Well, the one scout that I have talked with the most is a gentleman by the name of Denny Pacini, who lives in Kerman, California. Pacini was born in Italy, and came to the U.S. as a young man. He learned to speak English and wanted to play baseball. Like so many fathers did in those days, Pacini's father wanted him to be a farmer — these are the years following World War II. Minor league baseball paid about $60-$70 a month in those days. You sure weren't going to get fat and happy on that salary. Pacini convinced his dad that it was the right thing for him, and he signed to play. Unfortunately, he sustained a career ending injury, and was forced to turn his baseball career to scouting.

These days Pacini is scouting for the Los Angeles Angels. What makes his scouting job most interesting is where his duty takes him. In a few weeks, he will be heading for Africa. Because baseball talent is so scarce here in the the states, teams are looking for players in foreign countries. He has already covered many areas in Europe. There are so many high school and college players drafted each year by major league clubs, one wonders why the talent pool is lacking — it's just not there like it used to be. Many players and scouts of the past believe that the fundametals needed to play the game, as it was played in the 1960's and earlier, have not been taught properly.

The average player today is bigger and more physical than in the past, but lacks the fundamentals of the game — they simply are not being taught at the lower levels like they used to be. That said, I wonder about scouts like Pacini. What will they find in Russia or Africa? Pacini tells a story of giving 4-dozen baseballs to a group in Africa to practice with. After only 2 days they asked for more baseballs. Pacini asked the leader, "What happened to the balls I just gave you?" The leader replied, "They are hitting them in the woods outside of the play area." Pacini said, "Send guys into the woods to get balls." He was then told, "We do, but the monkeys grab them before we can get them." I guess we all have obstacles to overcome.

A Monopoly on the Field
MLB teams have to help

The National Football League has the greatest minor league system that could ever be imagined. All the great university and college players in the country are controlled, to some degree, by the NFL. Let's take the year 2005. Reggie Bush of the University of Southern California was named the best college football player in the nation. Can he play for the team of his choice? Not in the NFL. More than likely, he would be drafted by the worst team in the NFL.

He may want to play for New England, but he doesn't have that choice. That's why I call it a monopoly.

We know Reggie Bush did not end up in Houston, but at the time New Orleans was considered a pretty bad team. The player I can remember the most coming out of college and complaining about where he was drafted was quarterback John Elway. He wouldn't play for Baltimore, and a deal was made for him to go to Denver. The same thing happens in the National Basketball Association as well — the best college player has no say. The best player goes to one of the league's worst teams. They call it parity — I call it monopoly.

Baseball is the worst when it comes to controlling its game. The major league teams have developed what is called a farm system. The talent they get from high school and college is usually far from being major league caliber, so they are sent to the farm system to prepare. The classifications run from Single-A up to Triple-A. All players sent to these leagues are owned by the major league club the minor league team is affiliated with. The teams in each of these leagues are called franchises, and are individually owned by investors of each city. Now here is where the control comes in. The parent major league club tells each franchise team who they will receive as a player, sometimes sending along a manager of their choice, and they also pay their salaries.

It all sounds pretty good to this point. Let's take the franchise in Fresno, California, and see if you would like to be an investor. I worked in the front office of that Triple-A ballclub. In fact, I was called one of the founders and builders of this organization. In order to bring top minor league baseball back to Fresno, California, we had a lot of work to do. At one time Fresno had one of the top Single-A franchises in baseball. Unfortunately, a gentleman with a lot of money bought the franchise, and moved it. Fresno has a great baseball tradition. It gave the baseball world the likes of Frank Chance, Tom Seaver, Jim Maloney, Vic Lombardi, Dick Ellsworth and Dick Selma, to name just a few. Fresno deserved to have a professional baseball team. It's no small task to get a baseball franchise. Let's get into the nuts and bolts of bringing a Triple-A franchise to Fresno.

In 1993, I met John Carbray, and agreed to work with him. This journey began as a four-person team consisting of John, his wife Diane, Rick Finlay and myself. The initial step in the process is that we had to obtain a franchise — that was all John's expertise. John and Diane did not have the money to obtain the club, so investors had to be found. The investment money was obtained and a franchise was purchased at a cost of $7.2 million. Next, a stadium deal had to be negotiated at a cost of $48 million. To this point no cost had been applied to any major league team. John and Diane Carbray, now owners of the franchise, worked with the San Francisco Giants to create an affiliation. This only made sense since the earlier Fresno team had been with the Giants. Both sides agreed to terms, and the bond was formed with San Francisco. To this point Major League Baseball or the Giants haven't put up a dime. Is that proper simply because that's the way Major League Baseball has structured things?

What we wound up with in Fresno was a $48 million all-purpose stadium and a franchise, in the Giants, to work with at a cost of $7.2 million. That's quite an investment to get a ballclub on the field. Keep in mind that a major league team has the right to dictate what the facility should be like at no expense to that major league team. At the time the San Francisco Giants have no investment what-so-ever at a facility that they would train players to go to their big league roster. The players that were sent down were paid their salaries by the big league club. All other expenses were paid by the Fresno franchise. Uniforms, transportation, meal money on the road, to name a few, make up additional minor league club responsibility. The team also has a manager supplied by the Giants — you can bet the team is micro-managed by the Giants, and they oversee all transactions made. This is where the real control system kicks in.

The big leagues have a system called the disabled list. You hear a lot about the DL. In my opinion, some major league clubs really abuse this system. Let me give you an example of how this can work. Fresno has an outfielder going well and one of the players with the big club is going bad, so they declare him unfit to play for some reason. The reason can be fairly simple, like a torn fingernail or some other minor scrape, and he goes on the DL. From there the big club gets the player the Fresno fans have come to root for, and he's not replaced on the Fresno roster. This can happen a couple times a week, and the minor league team is forced to play with a short number of players. Sometimes, a pitcher has to play the outfield because two outfielders have been called up and the ballclub only had 4 to start with. The Giants own the players, so when they are called up a replacement should be added to the roster to remedy that problem.

Here is my solution to this problem the minor leagues face. It sure would be interesting if I was in the position like Branch Rickey, Jr., of the Pacific Coast League. I would create a rule that stated when any player is called up to the major leagues, he would have to be on that roster for 30 days. If he is returned, the player can then can only be called back at the end of the season. You might say, "Gus, that's penalizing the player." No, I don't believe it is. If a player gets a 30-day shot and can't make it, he deserves to be in the minors. That's why many players don't make it — they don't have the desire to push their ability to stay in the big leagues

Not all Triple-A teams have the same costs as the Fresno Grizzlies, but many do have high operating costs. I think the big league teams have some cost responsibility to the Triple-A franchise like a Fresno team. The cost of stadium is about $120,000 per month. I think the Giants, when they use the stadium from April until September, should pay $50,000 per month to have their players train there. Remember, it cost Fresno and the investors $45.2 million to get baseball, and it didn't cost Major League Baseball a dime — and they reap many rewards from the ballclub's existence. Minor league baseball often has to be creative in order to survive. They schedule other events in the stadium to make ends meet. Major League Baseball's monopoly of the game will make sure it stays that way.

If the Fresno franchise would have been managed properly over the years, perhaps I would not be writing this chapter. Don't get me wrong — it was baseball that gave me the opportunity to make a good living doing something I truly enjoy. I am not against Major League Baseball, but I do have the right to speak out about the things I believe. In my day there was no union to help represent me — to speak out on behalf of the players. Granted, there were few that may have made some headway on contracts, but they were the elite players and few and far between. In 1947, I was claimed on waivers by the Chicago White Sox, and sent to Hollywood of the Pacific Coast League where I signed a Hollywood contract. The big leagues did not have the monopoly they had today. The White Sox had an option. Chicago owned my contract and the big league minimum was $5,000 a year. I played for Hollywood under contract for over $7,000 a year at the time.

To keep baseball healthy, instruction at all levels needs to be knowledgeable and baseball savvy. I have heard it expressed by many former big league ballplayers, some of who are Hall of Fame members, that the game is a watered-down version of what used to be played. I believe this to be true also but for at least one major reason. To understand why this is happening one must look at how the system operates. Two places of baseball development are high school and college baseball programs. What is happening to this talent as it moves into the professional ranks? Top talent from schools don't get the right type of coaching and are often brought up to the big league roster before they are ready.

I believe the big league clubs ruin more talent than they develop in many systems. Go back a few decades and look at the talent that was brought up from the minors. Most players spent a few years in the minors learning to play baseball at a professional level. When they were ready they were sent up and had a much better chance to stay in the majors and become a factor. They did not have to endure this up and down exercise that is today's DL. Players are still learning baseball when they reach the big leagues, but there simply is not the amount of teaching and coaching that goes on in the minors. If you didn't get it there, you are certain to be in trouble when you reach the show.

Get rid of the Disabled List and leave the developing players in Triple-A and Double-A, until they are ready for the big leagues. And I will reiterate my belief that all major league clubs should have to pay their Triple-A clubs $50,000 a month during the playing season to defray stadium costs, the cost of the franchise, and the expense of helping to develop their players.

The Pension

Baseball owes the old-timers more than recognition

After World War II, the players and owners founded major league baseball's pension plan. It was a very simple plan in the beginning. If you had 5 years of service in the major league you became a vested member. If you stayed 10 years, you would collect $100 a month starting at the retirement age of 55. Mind you, that sounded pretty fair at that time. Remember, it was 1947 and the minimum salary was only $5000 per year. At the time this was put on paper we had no idea of what the cost of living would be in the years to come.

The 1960's saw the first baseball players union (Major League Baseball Players Association or MLBPA), and the players' salaries began to show the benefits of the union. With the union, the players' salaries and pension plans began to escalate rapidly. That was great for players of the 1970's forward, but many of the old timers, players that retired prior to 1970, and even fully vested players in the pension plan, were left behind. Greed became a major factor when Donald Fehr became the union leader and Peter Uberoth became commissioner of baseball. Now I say "greed" because the players of today, their union, and perhaps even some owners, have put a freeze on the old timers and what they get by way of the pension. The old timers are represented by the Major League Baseball Players Alumni Association (MLBPAA).

I bring this up simply to state this — players of today will get $90,000-$100,000 per year in their pension. I am all for that, but why are the players of the 1940's-1960's strapped with a frozen pension. Their pension should increase with the cost of living. No one had any idea players would be making $25,000,000 a year to play baseball and could add to their fund. We never had that opportunity.

Though I am glad to get a pension, I think of what it might have been, if we had been given the chance to grow with baseball. Players of the 1970's going back to 1947, receive about one-fourth of what the players of today get. The MLBPAA talk about this problem each year but seem to make no headway. We old timers don't want what the players of today get, just don't forget us. After all, the players of 1947 started the plan to begin with. Just take us along for a little bit of the ride. And there's no doubt that it could be done. That's why I call it greed. At the end of the day there is little or nothing out of the modern day player's pocket.

In the 1960's the average salary of a major league player was about $17,000 per year. Today, it is approaching $3,000,000 per year. Again, I say — more power to them. We just came along a little too soon. I am no lawyer and certainly not aware of all the legal ramifications of the pension plan, but I find it hard to believe that we old timers could not be helped with some type of cost-of-living clause. We don't want what today's players have, we'd just like what we deserve. Does all of this sound like sour grapes? Well, it certainly is not on my part. As I have mentioned earlier, I don't have a problem with the big dollars they earn. The players of today can buy an annuity that would pay them additional money per year, and I hope they are doing that.

Let me sum it all up this way — more power to the financial status of the players of today. Remember, it was the old timers who set the table. Unfortunately, most of the young players of today don't even know what's going on with the pension. We don't have a strong voice in the pension that is heard on a regular basis. No big agents are representing us and our interests. On the board there is John McHale, who I mentioned earlier, along with some other former ballplayers, many of whom I know. Doesn't seem to matter who though, they can't make Donald Fehr listen.

I have heard stories many times that the fund has excess money and they don't know what to do with it. If that's the case, let the Major League Baseball Players Alumni Association join the party. I am sure they could find some fine uses for the money, including taking care of the old timers.

Many unions of the past have killed the goose that laid the golden egg. I believe the players union, as we know it today, will do the same thing. And you can lump the agents of players in that very same category. When agents put a limit on how many pitches a pitcher can throw in a game, you have a problem — that's too much. There will come a point when agents will have the say on how many games a player can play per season. Probably one of my biggest complaints in this area is that the players of today and their agents could care less about the players that helped build the game and created the pension for them. That's called greed! Someday, maybe the MLBPAA will have their say and help the old timers. Until then, I'll say it again — we don't want what you have, we just want to share a little in what we helped you get.

FAMILY & FRIENDS

Family Ties
The wife and kids & baseball

Now there's a great question — "What is family life like in baseball?" I have often wondered what it was like for other players and their families that traveled as we did. I certainly know some of the difficulties that we faced, though I don't think many players are aware of all the problems their wives have to deal with during these travels. When you pack your bags for a two-week road trip, you leave your wife and kids, and join your baseball family. Many players with families look forward to road trips. It's a time you can be with your buddies, have dinner and a beer, share stories, and have an all-around good time. Meanwhile, the wife is home taking care of the kids.

Let me tell you a true-life story that nearly caused me to give up my baseball career during the 1955 season. I was with the Kansas City A's, and my wife, Gladys, was at our home in California. At the time, our second child, Gus, Jr., was on the way. We opened the season in April, and Gladys was to give birth in late May. I received word that the doctors would have to take the baby ahead of time, so I made arrangements with the ballclub to be with her in California. I missed a few games for the birth, then returned and continued to play. Unknown to me at the time, Gladys was heavily medicated. She was really having a tough time recovering.

While I was there I thought we had agreed that she would stay home with the children. If there were no problems, I would see her and the children at the end of the season. Late one night, I received a phone call from her. She was in Winslow, Arizona — kids in tow. Seems she had decided to bundle-up the little one, along with our 7-year old, Susan, and was trying to drive to Kansas City. I was completely taken by surprise. But that's only half of the story — what she said on the phone was really frightening. Gladys said she had stopped at a motel for the night and was being mistreated. She claimed they were shining bright lights in her room and trying to give her shock

That's me, on the opposite page, between two good friends at an old-timers game. Walker Cooper, a fine catcher, is on the left and slugger Hank Sauer is sporting the San Francisco colors.

135

treatments. At this point my surprise turned to fear, and my initial thought was to check to be sure the kids were in no danger. I didn't have a good feeling as she just pleaded with me to get there. Gladys believed her life was in danger. My imagination was running wild!

It was early morning, and my next call was to the Winslow Police. At this point at least my imagination had slowed, but all they would tell me was that my family was fine, and I should get there as soon as possible. I called our ballclub's business manager, got a flight out of Kansas City to Phoenix, and chartered a small plane to Winslow. That plane ride was a story in itself. It was early morning, the pilot was drunk, and the ride was rough — but we made it. I flagged a cab at the airport and headed to the motel. Arriving at the motel I received another in my long-line of surprises for the day. The police were there, and I assumed it was for Gladys — wrong! They were there on behalf of the motel.

Upon further investigation, it seems Gladys had taken quite a bit of medication. The long drive from California to Arizona was a little too much for her, and she temporarily lost her mind. In fact, she was giving her fair share of trouble to the motel, which resulted in the police presence. They ordered me to leave with my family. That was probably the best offer I had all day, so I took it. I drove to the exit of the motel and paused in the driveway for a moment. I took a deep breath knowing, if I made a right-hand turn I was headed back to California. After things had settled down a bit, I turned left and headed back to Kansas City to continue my career.

This was certainly, at least, part of the beginning of the end of my marriage. I later learned that Gladys had in some way gotten addicted to drugs and later became an alcoholic. I believe this was all related to the hard time she had bringing Gus, Jr., into the world. I continued my career in baseball, but could not keep the marriage together — 3 years later we were divorced. I will say at this time that it takes two to get together, and two to break it apart. I have no doubt I made many mistakes. I know Gladys hated spring training, and the long road trips. It was the way I had chosen to live my life, and there just wasn't anyway to make the marriage work any longer.

This is why I mentioned baseball and family. I am sure other players have similar stories because a ballplayer really does have two families — his wife and kids, and his baseball family. I certainly was never lonely, but at times had a little more excitement than I bargained for. I realize from first-hand experience that it takes a very strong, and understanding woman to be a baseball wife.

In the mid 1980's, Gus, Jr., found his mother in her apartment — she had passed on. I very seldom see my son, Gus Edward, Jr., — he was only 3-years old when his mother and I were divorced. I saw Little Gus, as we called him, a few times as a teenager. I was also at his wedding when he first married, but he chose to go his own way. He's a very successful businessman in the San Francisco Bay area. Unfortunately, as a father, I never had much opportunity to bond with him.

Friends

It's tough to see them all

My first year in Philadelphia, my wife and I, along with our 3-year old daughter, Susan, lived in a classic hotel in Germantown, Pennsylvania. I call it classic because it was built many years ago. Made of wood, it sported a porch that ran all the way around. The manager's name was Ken O'Brian and we became good friends. He treated my family great.

Ken told me he had tickets for the next game at which 4 of his friends and associates in the hotel business would be joining him. He had told them that he knew me, but they didn't believe him. The challenge, apparently, was now on, and Ken was out to prove he knew me the next night at the stadium. At Connie Mack Stadium when the game was over the fans would storm the field, wanting to touch the players or just to say "nice game" — pretty neat looking back on that.

On this night, Ken had informed his associates that when the game was over, they would run on the field and shake hands with me. Keep in mind that as players we knew all too well that we had to get off the field as quick as possible, because if you didn't you would get banged around, mostly by young fans. As I was headed towards the dugout I remember a gentleman grabbing me by the arm. I simply gave him one of those basketball style shoulder turns and raced into the dugout.

I took my shower and gathered my family together to head back to the hotel. As we entered the hotel, there was Ken and his 5 associates, everyone of them laughing. Well, you might have guessed. It was Ken that I had given the basketball shoulder turn to. I met his friends had a nice chat with them. I told a few stories and apologized to Ken. He had no idea what took place on the field after a game in Philadelphia. If you won the game and you got the visiting team out in the top of the ninth, it was always tough to get to the clubhouse. The fans wanted to congratulate and pat you on the back. That was all OK with me, but if you stopped on your way to the dugout, you could hardly get inside. That is what happened to Ken.

From Baseballs to Golf Balls

Good friends are always a blessing

When I first came to Fresno, one of the first people I met was a gentleman by the name of Hank Bocchini, Sr. Hank owned a driving range and a 9-hole golf course that you could play at night. Hank and I became fast friends and, needless to say, I was at his course many times. He gave me golf lessons and while he was an excellent teacher, I ended up being a less than fabulous student.

At the time, I was the sports director of a television station and when the big tournaments such as The Masters or The U.S. Open would be in town, I would get special credentials for Hank to attend. In turn, he would feed me special reports from each tourney. Worked out to be a pretty good all around.

Not only was Hank a good teacher, but he also had a pretty good golf game himself. He could certainly knock it around with the best of them. In addition to his driving range and golf course, he had a line of golfing slacks and shirts that did very well. Some of the golf pros of the '60s and '70s used his line of golfwear. Years later when Hank passed away, I continued my friendship with his family. Hank, Jr., is a very fine young man, and he and his wife, Nancy, gave us Dan, a third generation.

When Senior passed on, his son continued on with the business and has done very well. I see their family very often and still work on my game, trying improve striking that little round ball — and continue to get humbled. I tell this story simply to say how nice it is to have good times to share with great friends.

Folks in My Life

People who made a difference for me

I just wanted to list a few of the people who really influenced my life over the years. This list could be quite a bit longer, but I have tried to keep it very brief. For the record, my Dad and Mom, with my 3 sisters and 3 brothers, would top the list.

Raymond Alford

He was my football and basketball coach in high school and taught me how to be a competitor and a winner. To me, he was more than just my coach. With my Dad passing away when I was only 15, he became like a second father to me. My entire family had a true love for Coach Alford. Along with Mom and Dad, he taught me the right things to strive for in life. After his teaching and coaching days at Beaumont High School, he became superintendent of all schools in the area.

U. S. Navy Officers

This one goes out to all my commanding officers. In 1942, I joined the Navy, and while many did not make it home, I was one of the fortunate ones who did. In 1945 I was given an honorable discharge, and I just want to say thanks to many who helped bring me back home safely.

Ki Ki Cuyler

In 1946, my first year in baseball after the World War II, I reported to the Atlanta Crackers of the Southern Association. This was Double-A baseball at the time. I had been in Class-D ball before the war, and Cuyler remembered me as a 180-pound speedster. When I showed up that spring, I was a strapping 230-pounder — quite a change! He took 10 pounds off me with a fungo bat, as I chased balls all over the park, and he taught me how to get in shape.

Jimmie Dykes

A Hall of Famer in my book, Jimmie Dykes, was my manager when I reported to Hollywood of the PCL in 1947. He was what you would call "a players manager." He seldom got on the players, but would practice teaching when mistakes were made. Jimmie led the Hollywood club in 1947 and 1948, then moved to the Philadelphia Athletics. There, he would be groomed to take over for baseball legend Connie Mack, when he retired. He liked the long ball and that's probably one reason that we got along so well. I was with Jimmie many times during my pro ball days in the minor leagues as well as with Philadelphia and Detroit in the big leagues.

Big League Teammates

Over my big league baseball career, I have had many good teammates. This is by no means a complete list for me; nonetheless, some of the best were Dave Philley, Nelson Fox, Eddie Robinson, Luke Appling, and managers, Ted Lyons, Jack Onslow and Paul Richards. I have some great memories of our trainer, Packy Swartz, as well. A couple of folks from the Chicago White Sox I will never forget are Frank Lane, our general manager, and the owner, young Chuck Comiskey.

Moving over to the Philadelphia Athletics, first and foremost, would be Connie Mack, and his two sons, Earle and Roy. Eddie Joost, Pete Suder and Ferris Fain, the great double-play combination, were sure exciting to play behind. Bobby Shantz was always a pleasure to play with and be around. Joe Astroth, Ray Murray, Joe Coleman and Dick Fowler were also fine fellows. Moving to Detroit I'd say Frank Lary, Jim Bunning and Paul Foytack on the hill, with Al Kaline, Charlie Maxwell, Johnny Groth and Tom Morgan in the field — all great guys to play with.

Joe DeMaestri

Joe and I became friends when he joined the A's in Philadelphia. He became a member of the club just before we moved to Kansas City. We roomed together on some of the road trips, and after games we often had dinner. I remember him buying a pack of cigarettes at a high-class restaurant in New York once. I grabbed his $20 bill and told the girl to keep the change. I think that was the biggest tip Joe ever gave. We play in golf tournaments from time-to-time and enjoy seeing each other when we get the chance.

Tom Morgan

Tom and I became good friends both on and off the baseball field. I remember a game in New York when Tom was a member of the high-powered Yankees team. I told him, "The first time I bat today, I am going to bunt on you." I don't think he believed me, but I wasn't fooling around one bit. Sure enough, it happened — I bunted on him and beat it out right there in Yankee Stadium.

Jerry Hatfield

I broke my right collarbone in 1949, while playing in Cleveland. I was with the Chicago White Sox at the time. I tried to make a diving/rolling catch of a line-drive and I didn't complete the roll. I was out for the better part of the season, and during the winter I joined a health club owned by my good friend, Jerry Hatfield. He worked on my shoulder all winter so I could play in 1950. Jerry was a big part in my baseball career.

After Baseball

Starting a new life after baseball I met the Sims family. Ed and Betty had two beautiful daughters, Marla and Sandy. Sandy married Rex Babcock, and they have three children. Luckily for me, I married Marla and now, some 45 years later, she is still Mrs. Zernial. We live in Clovis, California.

Lloyd Merriman

A great athlete, but a greater friend. Lloyd would do anything, at anytime, for his friends. The baseball field at Clovis High is named in his honor.

Radio and Television

My second profession made leaving baseball a little easier as time passed. Guys like Roger Rocka, Chuck Carson, Karen Humphrey, John Wallace, Chuck Hoover, Lee Jason, Lee Jensen, Dick Carr, Al Radka and Angelo Stalis are just a few of the names from the industry that helped make my career and life such a pleasant experience in Fresno.

Automobile Dealers and Personnel

Dan Day, owner of Dan Day Pontiac, was both my boss and my friend. Len Fraser, Ed Burns and John Solem are guys I spent many a day on the golf

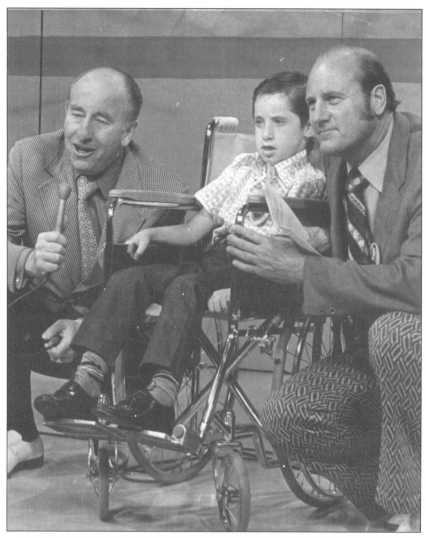

That's Al Radka and I doing a little on the air charity work. I have always enjoyed giving some help to those who were less fortunate.

course with. Swanson-Fahrney Ford included Russ Noble, Don Fahrney, Jerry and his son. Then there was Ray Decker Ford — Ray was a good man and, like Dan Day, sure did a lot of good work in the community.

Roger Rocka

Roger is certainly a true friend. Since he moved away to live in the northwest, I really miss him. Roger was the news director, while I was the sports director at Channel 30 for many years. We spent time together on many occasions between our news shows. I talked for hours sharing my stories on baseball, and he would tell me of his experiences in broadcasting. He was really an influential factor in my writing this book.

Al Radka

Al was a one-man band — a salesman and comedian of sorts, as well as a real legend in the San Joaquin Valley. When I first met him, I had just joined the broadcast team at KFRE. He had been president of the student body at Fresno State University, and had played 3 years as a lineman on the football team, earning All-Coast each of his 3 seasons. I worked on many charity events with Al who was best known as Mr. Fresno.

Buford Karracker, G.L. Johnson and Gene Sperling

Buford led me to the Lord — Pastors Johnson and Sperling keep me on the right road.

Tom Sommers

When I met Tom I knew he was a unique and special person. Tom had a tough childhood, but he became a devout follower of the Lord and shares his testimony with many people. Tom played football and baseball at Fresno State University, as well as some professional baseball. He spent 10 years in the front office of the California Angels. Tom has many friends and always seems to find time for each and everyone.

Hal Britton

Hal is a special person in my life. There is an old expression in war-time that asks, "Who would you like to have with you in a foxhole?" My answer would surely be, Hal Britton. Hal was a member of the Fresno Police for 30 years, and his last few years of service were as the Chief of Police of Fresno. I first met Hal when I came to Fresno to play an exhibition game in 1950, as I had joined an all-star team led by Bob Feller. We played a black all-star team that was led by Luke Easter. Our club had some pretty good talent including Bob Feller and Mike Garcia on the mound, with Lloyd Merriman, Enos Slaughter and myself patrolling the outfield. Hal Britton was our catcher. When I moved to Fresno in 1961, Hal had joined the police department. As time went on we tried to get together as much as possible and shared many good times. In those days the police had a pretty good baseball team, too. I played a few games with them. Looking back, we were pretty good at baseball and lunch (ha-ha), but when we hit the golf course we were a couple of real hackers!

Above I am receiving the 2007 Al Radka Award and on the left is my good friend Hal Britton.

On the opposite page, It's 1961 and that's me with my beautiful new bride, Marla and son, Jim. Those were the good ole days of the beginning of my second family as well as second career. They both worked out just fine!

5 DECADES IN FRESNO

The Home Town Team
Making Fresno my home

After retiring from baseball in 1959, I was living in Los Angeles with no intent of making that my home. After 16 years of professional baseball, it was time for me to figure out just what I was qualified to do and just what was life after baseball going to be for me. I took real honest look at myself and felt that I was qualified for absolutely nothing at all. Talk about a real eye-opener of self-reflection! Players of my day typically had little to fall back on. It is probably different for today's players with the increased salaries they enjoy.

It just so happens that I met a gentleman who offered me a job with a stock and bond firm. I accepted and started learning the business at an accelerated rate. I picked up just enough to get by, but sometimes that's just not enough. Early on it seems I sold a gentleman's stock late one day — the next day, it was one-half point higher. I got beat-up pretty good for that miscue. He thought I should have known better and maybe I should have, but this was a new gig for me. I didn't feel I was making much headway as a stockbroker and a career move seemed the best choice.

I didn't really feel after the 1959 season with Detroit that I was ready to hang-up my baseball career. I thought that I may be able to catch on with a team, somewhere. I was divorced at the time with kids and very little money in the bank. I had to find employment quickly. I called the Detroit club to see if there were any opportunities with them. Unfortunately, there was nothing for me in Detroit. My next thought was to contact the Dodgers who were playing in the Coliseum in Los Angeles. There was a very short left field porch there. I talked with Buzzie Bavasi about playing, but he didn't offer me a contract. However, he wanted to take me to spring training at Vero Beach, Florida. I declined his offer. Looking back, I believe I should have taken it though. I know I could still play at that time, and I could have been a productive player on that ballclub. A couple of teams in the PCL offered to sign me, but by that time I had decided to retire for good. I think there will always be a part of me that feels I should have continued. I'm sure many players feel that way.

During the off-season of 1959, I met Marla Jean Sims in Los Angeles. Truth be told, I was completely turned upside down by her beauty and charm.

I think this photo shows just how pleased I was with the new direction of my life at the beginning of the 1960's. Marla and I had just gotten married and I couldn't have been any happier — things were looking up.

We began dating and things were really falling into place for me. Meeting Marla was certainly a major factor in my decision to give up baseball. I saw this as an opportunity to begin an entirely new career. I met Marla at a restaurant while I was in the stock business. A friend of mine, by the name of Hodemaker, owned a chain of these restaurants called Hody's. We were together almost everyday after that. She was a single mom with a young son, James. She had been divorced after a very short marriage. I left the security business and was now doing some public relations work for a west coast glass distributor. What I really had in mind, though, was a new career in radio broadcasting.

Over the years, I had become friends with many of the play-by-play announcers for the teams I had played for. There was Byrum Saam in Philadelphia and Merle Harmon in Kansas City to name a couple. Harmon later went on to work with Bob Uecker in Milwaukee. Driven to get into the broadcast industry, I met with Harmon and asked him for advice on breaking into the field. Harmon suggested I go to a smaller market than Los Angeles to get started. I took his advice, packed up my new bride Marla, and headed for Fresno, California.

Let me digress for just a moment. The public relations work I had been doing was for National Auto Glass, a company based in Los Angeles. I had made a couple trips to Fresno as the representative for that company. As luck would have it, they were looking for a new owner — it all fit perfectly. I became part-owner of the glass shop and found myself in the smaller market I was looking for to begin my broadcasting career. And in all honesty, it wasn't luck at all — the Lord was at work in my life. I didn't know it at the time, but I did come to understand it later. During this time, Marla was not happy with all the changes that were going on. She was a gamer, as they say in baseball, and stuck with me though. She understood what I was trying to do. Marla was unhappy because she missed seeing her family. She was very close to her parents and her sister. Her sister Sandy, had 3 children that she had developed very close bonds with. Here in Fresno she had no friends and, with a young son, it was very difficult at times. Being like many men, my thoughts were on starting over and making a living for the person I loved. It was an easier change for me because I knew some people in Fresno. I had played in an all-star exhibition game in Fresno with Bob Feller, against Luke Easter's all-star club in 1950. I met Lloyd Merriman, who lived in Fresno, as well as

Hal Britton, who later became the police chief. It was Merriman that helped us find a place to live. The entire process was rough going, but I had a small job and felt my new career was getting off the ground.

I was trying to use my baseball name to get acquainted with some of the local radio stations. I was lucky enough to meet some of the people at KFRE radio — there was also KFRE television. I made a deal with the station that I would do five minutes of sports on the radio, mornings and evenings, and they would give me advertising spots for my glass company. I arrived in Fresno ready to go in April of 1961. It was then that I found out not many people knew who Gus Zernial was, or that he had ever played pro ball. It was an entirely new and challenging world for me. The new Zernial family was up for the challenge though.

I had enjoyed 16 years in professional baseball and was paid fairly well for those days. I had owned 3 different homes over that period and now was embarking on a second family, second career and new life, all at one time. I was ready to climb the ladder to success all over again. It was the summer of 1961 — I was 38 years old and not looking back for second. It was rough at times, but Marla and I stood up straight and faced each challenge head-on.

In September of 1961, Marla became pregnant. I felt I was beginning to gain some ground now, laying a nice foundation for the future. I had 2 children from my previous marriage, Susan Carol and Gus, Jr., and they remained my responsibility. I tried to see them as often as I could, but their mother made it difficult at times. For several years, I even lost track of them. Still, they remained my responsibility and, thank the Lord, Marla stood by me through it all. Marla's son, Jim Cavell, was 4-years old and that April, it was full steam ahead for the Gus, Marla and Jim team — a new beginning for us all. Jim took my name and became James Zernial — Fresno, California became our home. In May of 1962, Marla made me the proud father of a beautiful baby girl. We named her Lisa Marlane. At that time, I still owned National Auto Glass, but I was making some excellent contacts in the broadcasting industry. By late 1963, things were really turning around for me.

Though on the whole things were looking up for me, I was having trouble keeping up with the competition in my glass business. I decided to sell my company to a larger glass company. San Joaquin Glass was owned by Harvey McHenry. I was then hired by Mr. McHenry. Not only did I work for him, but I became a family friend. While working for his glass company, I met some of the finest people one could imagine in the auto and insurance field. Many are still my friends today. I became the sales manager, and that meant a little more salary, which was great.

With San Jauquin Glass, I was an outdoor salesman and developed new auto glass business. If anyone is wondering what I did as a salesman, I'll tell you — replace broken plate glass windows in commercial buildings, broken windshields and door glass in all types of automobiles, and installing glass in all commercial buildings. And those are just a few examples of what the business entailed. I remember one Pontiac dealership that had problems with water spots on the glass. It seems that this dealer's maintenance man would turn the sprinklers on early in the morning to water the grass. Obviously, the water gets on all the cars and, before they could be wiped down, it would dry and spot all of the glass. The owner, Herman Theroff, spent quite a bit of money trying to overcome this problem. One day he called and asked for my solution. I said to them send me some cars with spots on the glass, and I would see what I can do. Wow, from a pro ball player to spot-solver on car glass — if that doesn't beat all! Fortunately, I found a secret weapon. There was an old general store that sold bars of Bonami Soap — A wet rag and a little soap, and the spots were gone. So, I charged him so much per car, and we had a nice little business deal. Well, that was my business at that time, but, remember, glass was not to be my final stop.

The many people I met in the glass business were just as important to me as the many I met on the baseball field. I have always felt that every person you meet in the passing years of your life has something to offer. In turn, those you meet may take from you something they can use in their life. I'm sure I speak to many that could never hit a curve ball, but I may say something that will help them handle their next curve, whatever it may be. In the meantime, I was working with the announcers that were doing play-by-play football and basketball for KFRE — Hal McWilliams and Bob Fulton. I worked as the color man with Hal and Bob for about a year. Then in 1964, I was hired as the radio sports director and, a short time later, moved up to sports director for both the radio and television sides. By this time, I was out of the glass business.

At KFRE, the radio and television were both owned by the same folks.

My career in radio and television was really fantastic. Here I am doing the sports on KFRE and really enjoying my job.

The radio side presented a bid to do all the sports for Fresno State College. This meant that I had to learn quickly the play-by-play aspects of football, basketball, baseball and all other sports. Fresno State was a member of the CCAA Conference. I put in quite a few hours listening to other announcers and their play-by-play styles. I would spend a lot of preparation time for a game — it was time well spent and I got to be pretty good at my new profession. It was great fun for me to travel to each college campus, doing the broadcast of each sporting event. My family was now growing up, and Marla was trying to get used to me being gone for much of the time. Here again, like many men, I was enjoying my career, but the wife and youngsters didn't quite understand. Lisa was now going on 4, and Jim was soon to be 9-years old.

The time and effort were now paying off as I had entered the new profession that I had moved to Fresno for. And make no mistake — I wanted to be the best I could be in the radio and television field. I was a little rough and unpolished in the beginning, but I improved each time out. I wanted to be like Byrum Saam or Merle Harmon — well maybe not that good, but good enough to get to the big leagues. As a youngster I had dreamed of being a big league player, and now I was dreaming in the same way about broadcasting. During my radio years I had the opportunity to interview some of the greatest athletes of all-time — hall of famers in track and field, baseball, football and many other sports. Fresno was certainly a hot-bed for sports. The Fresno Athletic Hall of Fame doesn't take back seat to any other city hall of fame in the country. There are over 200 members and over 30 are nationally and internationally recognized. Each year they hold a hot-stove dinner to honor past and present athletes, and it is a truly fine event.

By now, Marla and I were getting used to Fresno — it was becoming home. James and Lisa were growing up quickly it seemed, and making many new friends in school. Things had all come together very nicely for me in my new life — I felt I had made it again!

In 1969, things were happening at the station, and I had a big decision to make. Cap Cities, the company that owned both stations, sold the radio side of the business. I chose to stay with the company, and moved into television completely. KMJ picked up the radio contract to do all the Fresno sports. Bill Woodward became the voice of the Fresno State Bulldogs and, to this day, is still on the job. He has been truly outstanding over the years.

I became sports director at KFRE and in that position, worked with some great people. That group was so talented that we were the number one rated news team in the market. Roger Rocka was news director and anchorman. Chuck Carson was the weather man (and had a great personality). Al Radka was "Mr. Everything," including his own show and hosting movies. By 1970, we had settled down completely and were thinking of buying a home. James was now 13-years old and Lisa was 8. Jim was a good athlete, playing football, baseball and basketball. Lisa was involved in gymnastics and was very talented. When we arrived in Fresno, the population was 150,000 — today it's over 450,000! Now that's real growth!

I had a nice little run at the station, but in January of 1976, I decided to leave television to explore other fields. My popularity among the people of the San Joaquin Valley had grown due to my exposure on radio and television over the years. From 1976 to 1990, I was doing commercials for auto dealers, as well as sales. This all led me to becoming part of the team that founded and built the multi-purpose stadium in Fresno.

Looking back now, I believe that leaving my position as the sports director at KFRE Channel 30 was a mistake. I was going to be taking on the challenges of the advertising field, and I was simply not prepared for the obstacles ahead. I had joined Hovland Advertising and had received very little help or guidance — I was lost in the woods to be quite honest. I was doing commercials for Dan Day Pontiac at the time. I left Hovland to work for the Pontiac Agency as a fleet and lease manager, and continued to do commercials for them. This was all happening in 1976. My family was my main concern at that time.

Jim had just completed high school and was getting ready for college. He graduated from McLane High School, where he played 3 sports — football, baseball and basketball. My wife and I spent many enjoyable days in the bleachers, watching him play. He was a good football player, but received no scholarship offers from any major colleges. He suffered through mononucleosis which was a great setback. He went on to play one year of junior college football, though, he chose not to pursue the athletic world.

Jim is unmarried at this time and has 2 children — a son Eziekiel and a stepdaughter, Brandi, who has two children. He went to work for the Pepsi Cola Bottling Company and spent over 30 years with them before retiring on disability. He had a bad accident and became disabled when he broke his back. The company has made it difficult to reach any kind of a settlement.

Lisa was about to begin high school at Clovis West where my oldest daughter, Susan, was teaching. Lisa was a real prankster in those days and teased her stepsister quite a bit. Susan had worked her way through college and earned her degree in Education. Lisa was very popular in high school and was a cheerleader. She was also a talented gymnast, and I clearly remember her mother and I worrying about her on the balance beam and uneven bars. She graduated from high school in 1980. In addition to her high school activities, Lisa did some modeling work.

Lisa married at a young age and became a very successful homemaker and mother. She has 4 children, Afton, Adam, Adison and Ryan. Her husband, Barry Pearlstein, is a very successful businessman. He, too, was a very good athlete. He played college football and still, at 43 years old, is a good softball player. Barry is not only a son-in-law, but also a great friend. He has done so much for Marla and I, as well as many of his other friends. He's just a good guy. Their family has really grown up nicely over the years. Afton, their oldest daughter, has her own daughter named Jaedyn.

We see our children and grand children often — Marla and I are very proud of our family. While we love them all very much, we have sort of a special feeling for our great grandchild, Jaedyn. She is only a couple of years old, but charms everyone she comes in contact with.

Holy Cow

My Harry Carey encounter

I added this short story to this section, because it follows the part of the book that covers my journey into the field of radio and television. I felt this was the perfect place to show some of the difficulties one encounters when entering this highly competitive profession.

I guess many baseball people have a Harry Carey story. Harry was a part of the game for so many years that, if you spent any amount of time at the various ball parks around the league, you probably bumped into him. Here's my encounter with the Hall of Fame announcer.

As a young big league player I had the pleasure of meeting Harry, though I don't recall what team he was broadcasting for at the time. Long after I left baseball, and well into my own broadcasting career, I received a call from the Chicago White Sox front office. They wanted me to interview for a job with the White Sox broadcasting team. Harry Carey and another pretty good broadcaster by the name of Milo Hamilton made up the team at that time.

As fate would have it, just as I was checking into the hotel in Arlington, Texas, the first guy I ran into was Harry. We greeted each other in a cordial fashion, and then Harry says, "I know why you are here, but I can't help you." Well, I was sort of taken back by that greeting. At the time I didn't know what to make of it. It was only later that found out why I received such a strange comment from him.

The Chicago organization had asked me to meet them for their series, with the Texas Rangers in Arlington, for the purpose of doing a pre-game show and then sitting in the booth for a couple of innings. This was late in the 1975 season. As I recall, I did the pre-game show as scheduled. It was a two-man booth, so I sat behind Milo and Harry. If you are doing play-by-play, you're always prepared with a scorecard and as much additional information as possible. I was not prepared with any supporting material when Harry handed me the microphone. Talk about being hung out to dry. I tried to fake it, but in a situation like that I just butchered the play-by-play — I never stood a chance. A more experienced person, who knew Harry and understood the situation better, would have told him what to do with the microphone. I was really taken back by the entire experience.

The next day I got the line-up from Don Drysdale, who was the voice of the Texas Rangers at the time. I did a couple of innings that I thought went pretty well — nonetheless, I didn't stay for the third day. I had my young daughter Lisa with me and felt I had dealt with enough frustration for one trip. We caught a flight back to Fresno. Harry had made it quite clear that he didn't want me there. I have no doubt whatsoever that he purposely set me up to fail that day.

At the time this all occurred, though, I hadn't been written off completely. I was again scheduled to meet with some of the front office people from the White Sox ballclub at the World Series in Oakland. The A's had won the American League title that year. I got my hotel room at the American League headquarters and looked for the White Sox group that I was scheduled to meet with. They may have been there, but I never saw them. I did, however, meet with Frank Lane, the general manager when I played with the Sox in 1949 and 1950. He had traded me to the Philadelphia A's in 1951. Frank had some very kind words for me that I really appreciated. He also congratulated me on getting the broadcasting job with our old team. Now there was a surprise to me. I watched the ball games in Oakland and then headed home. Never did see any of the Chicago group in Oakland. I really wasn't sure what to make of the entire situation.

When I got back to Fresno, I continued my position as Sports Director at KFRE television. About a month later I received a call from the White Sox. They informed me that I wasn't going to be offered the broadcasting position I had auditioned for. I thanked them for the opportunity, and that was the last I heard from the White Sox. However, that was not the last I would hear of Harry Carey.

The following spring, I was sent to Phoenix, Arizona, to cover some of spring training for KFRE television, a CBS affiliate. While I was there, I ran into an old broadcast buddy that had lived in the Chicago area. I was completely surprised by what he asked me at the time. I believe his words to me were, "What in the world did you do to Harry Carey?" Seems that Harry had a radio show during the off-season, and he bad-mouthed me for the entire winter. Now that sure gave me a little insight on why I didn't make the White Sox broadcast team. I realize that it was possible that I simply wasn't qualified — but after hearing this I figured Harry may have had something to do with it.

Harry was a pretty good broadcaster, and he even made the Hall of Fame as one. He deserves that recognition, but he sure failed miserably in my book when it comes to human relations. Needless to say, my feelings toward Mr. Harry Carey changed quite a bit after that.

There's No Place Like Home
People of Fresno, California

After retiring from baseball to Fresno, I found the area to be a hot-bed of talent. Many former professional athletes from many sports were there, and there were also many loyal fans that followed these athletes.

There have been so many kind people that have opened doors for us upon our arrival. Tom Meehan, a sportswriter for the *Fresno Bee*, wrote a big article in the paper of my arrival to Fresno and how I was going to make it my home. Wow — was that ever a door opener!

Pete Mehas was coach at Edison High and later became principal of Clovis High, and then the superintendent of Fresno County Schools. Pete was a former star player on the Fresno State football team. He joined me in the radio booth on some of my FSU football game broadcasts. He was instrumental in getting me into the Fresno Athletic Hall of Fame, a group that has over 30 nationally and internationally known athletes — truly unique in its category.

I have been fortunate enough to have many radio and television personalities and call them friends. Guys like Al Radka, Roger Rocka, Don Elliot and many more became very close to me. Also from the auto industry I have enjoyed the friendships of Dan Day, Ray Decker and the Fahrney family, to name just a few.

When you sit down to write, so many friends come to mind that have played such an important part in your life. When you try to name a few, you find out there were hundreds. They are all important, but some you have to mention as I have. Bufe Karraker, who led me to the Lord, and G.L. Johnson are both fine men of God and super pastors.

These are some of the men of my new beginning here in Fresno, with many more to follow. In my baseball world there are numerous people and here are a few. Pete Bieden and Bob Bennett of the Fresno State coaching staff, Jim Maloney, Dick Ellsworth, Vic Lombardi, Dick Selma and Jack Hanna. A man that I can truly call a friend from this baseball world is Tom Sommers. Tom worked in the front office of the California Angels for over 10 years. We share many good memories. A Fresno Hall of Fame player in softball, Hal Britton, is a real buddy. To all my friends of Fresno — thank you.

The Fresno Connection
The place for us to be

At this point I have lived in Fresno for almost 50 years. It's true that I was born and raised in Beaumont, Texas, and spent 14 years in Los Angeles, but Fresno is still home sweet home. In addition to being home, Fresno has given me many great business opportunities, as well as a chance to make many friends along the way.

Baseball, radio and television gave me the opportunity to speak at service clubs, and other organizations throughout the valley region. Doors were opened, allowing me to work with some of the best folks in the auto dealership field at that time. Dan Day Pontiac, Decker Ford and Swanson-Fahrney Ford, to name just a few. Each of their families welcomed me and my family with open arms. I became good friends with so many in that industry. We spent many a morning or afternoon on the golf course knocking that little white ball around. The competition was pretty intense at times — they always wanted to beat me, but if I had anything to say about it that wasn't going to happen.

The Fresno Athletic Hall of Fame has really given me some great memories over the years. Numerous superb athletes are from Fresno, many known all over the United States, even the world. In track and field there is Dutch Warmerdam, who coached at the University of Fresno. Dutch was pole-vaulter and held the record for many years. He did his vaulting the old-fashioned way — with a bamboo pole. Along came the improved poles, and the record quickly went over 15 feet. Bob Mathias was a two-time Olympic Decathlon Champion. After his track and field days, he made several movies and then became a member of the U.S. Congress. And who could forget Rafer Johnson — Olympic Decathlon Champion?

In Football there's Trent Dilfer, who led Baltimore Ravens to a Super Bowl victory. Heisman Trophy runner-up, David Carr was drafted number one by Houston. There's also a pretty good stable of coaches including Daryl Rogers, Jim Sweeney and Pat Hill. Many of their players have gone on to enjoy successful National Football League careers.

Fresno has contributed to auto racing as well, boasting some of the world's best drivers. First and foremost in my book is Billy Vucovich. This

This photo was taken after my induction into the Fresno Athletic Hall of Fame — it was quite an honor for me.

two-time winner at Indianapolis was known as the driver that changed racing at the Old Brickyard. Sadly, Billy was killed at the speedway in the early 1950's. Then came his son, Billy, Jr., who qualified many times but never was able to win there. I often see Billy, Jr. on the golf course. He had a son that came up in the racing world and was also killed racing in midget cars as a very young driver. He was being groomed for Indy — I guess it's just in their blood. Johnny Boyd qualified 13 years in a row at Indy. Though he was never a winner there, he finished in the top 10 many times. Speaking of racing, anyone that spent time around Fresno from the 1940's through the 1960's could never forget the great times at the Kearney Bowl and the hardtop racing. The battles between Al Pombo and Marshall Sargent are legendary. Marla and I are great friends with Bill and Barbara Weaver, and the four of us did all we could to attend those fabulous races at Kearney.

Fresno had its share of top notch boxers and bowlers, as well. In boxing Wayne Thorton fought for the light-heavyweight championship in New York. Mack Foster had it out with Muhammad Ali — both came out on the short end of the fight, but they were top-notch boxers just the same. The most memorable fighter, in my opinion, was Young Corbett III, as he was known. He was a world champion in the welterweight division. Corbett and I spent quite a bit of time at the pool tables at Cedar Lanes. Corbett's real name was Ralph Giordano. Cedar Lanes was owned by Spalding Wathen — he was a true bowling fanatic. He sponsored the bowling tour for several years, and the fans of Fresno got to see some top-notch bowlers. The likes of Earl Anthony and Bill Weber really put a charge into the crowds and the pins.

When it comes to my sport, Fresno could really turn them out, and, for some reason, many were top pitchers. Tom Seaver went to high school in Fresno and then to the University of Southern California. He finished up his career in the bigs winning more than 300 games and topped that off with an induction into the Baseball Hall of Fame. Then, there was Jim Maloney, a 12-year veteran who pitched most of his career with Cincinnati Reds. He chalked up almost 200 wins and had three no-hitters to his credit. Jim played on the same high school team as Dick Ellsworth, another major league pitcher. At that time in high school, Dick was the starting pitcher and Jim played shortstop. Maloney was a pretty good hitter too. Fresno high schools Roosevelt and Bullard produced more than their share of baseball talent. If they didn't go

Above I am hamming it up for the camera with a couple of pretty tough guys — professional boxers George Foreman on the left and Mack Foster to the right.

To the right are Bill and Barbara Weaver, our great friends and Kearney Bowl race day companions.

FROM THE OFFICE OF
MAYOR ALAN AUTRY

PROCLAMATION

WHEREAS, GUS ZERNIAL (a.k.a. Ozark Ike) was born on June 27, 1923. He was a professional baseball player for 16 years, and from 1949-59 was in the Major Leagues with the White Sox, Athletics and the Tigers. Before joining the U.S. Navy in December, 1941, he hit .336 with the Cardinals Minor League at age 18; and

WHEREAS, Gus led the Major Leagues in 1951 with 129 RBI and 33 homeruns, ahead of Hall-of-Famer Ted Williams in both categories. He hit more homeruns than Yogi Berra, Mickey Mantle, and Ted Williams from 1950-57 with 220 round-trippers and in 1953 was the American League All-Star starting leftfielder. Gus' Major League record (one that San Francisco Giants outfielder Barry Bonds recently tied), was 7 homeruns in just 4 games at the beginning of the 1951 season (2 against the New York Yankees, 4 against the St. Louis Browns, and 1 against the Detroit Tigers). He was recently inducted into the Detroit Tigers Wall of Fame in Comerica Park and to the Philadelphia Baseball Hall of Fame for his time spent with the Philadelphia Athletics; and

WHEREAS, Gus has been with the Grizzlies since 1993, selling season tickets before there was a proposed stadium and even before there was a team. Gus is an active participant with the Grizzlies front office. The power-hitting star of the 50's is now hitting homeruns with baseball fans throughout the Central San Joaquin Valley; and

WHEREAS, Gus is often a guest speaker with several civic clubs sharing his experiences in the Major Leagues as well as keeping the community informed about the downtown stadium.

NOW, THEREFORE, BE IT RESOLVED that I, Alan Autry, Mayor of the City of Fresno, do hereby proclaim Wednesday, June 27, 2001, to be:

"GUS ZERNIAL DAY"

in the City of Fresno. Gus will reach the well earned and respected age of 78 years young, and is a true inspiration to us all. Happy Birthday Gus!!

IN WITNESS WHEREOF, I have hereunto set my hand and affixed the Seal of the City of Fresno, California, this 27th day of June, 2001.

MAYOR ALAN AUTRY

It's quite an honor to be recognized in your community to the level I have been. The document above is a prized possession of mine that proclaims "Gus Zernial Day" in Fresno. It was given by Mayor Alan Autry on June 27, 2001. These are the type of things that make all the hard work most worthwhile.

directly into professional ball, they often chose to play for Pete Bieden or Len Bourdett at Fresno City Junior College. Continuing with my baseball hit list there was Vic Lombardi who pitched for Brooklyn and Pittsburgh. The first time I saw Lombardi he started a spring game against the Chicago White Sox in Southern California. I thought he was the batboy, and guess what — he beat us that day. I later met him in Fresno when he was teaching golf. We were good friends for 37 years, until his passing. Truman Clevenger was a 7-year veteran who played with Washington, Boston and New York of the American League. These days he owns a Ford-Lincoln dealership in Porterville, California. Truman was an All-American pitcher with the University of Fresno. You can also add Dick Selma and Jeff Weaver to the list, but I'm sure there many others I've missed.

I had the pleasure of playing golf with Jerry Heard and Bill Glasson. Both of these fellows have more than 10 years of experience on the PGA Tour. I can't forget my friend on the LPGA, either — Shelly Hamlin. In softball we have the Fresno Rockets — Gloria May and Jean Contel — both were All-Americans.

What I have tried to accomplish in this chapter is recognizing the people that have helped make Fresno what it is today. Many of these folks have also made our time here in Fresno so special and enjoyable — the Weaver family, the Britton family, Tom Sommers and family, John Carbray family and the Gorman family... I could go on and on. The people I have met, coupled with my baseball, and radio and television experiences, have been the true inspiration behind the composition of the script for this book.

A Life Altering Experience
You gotta have heart

Life in Fresno has been fabulous, but there are always those times, no matter where you live, that you have to keep the faith. I experienced one of those events when, on June 7, 2005 — I had a heart attack. I was taken by ambulance to Community Hospital in Fresno where it was discovered that one of my main arteries was almost 100% clogged. This took place on June 8, the day following the heart attack. A procedure was done to clear the artery, and a stint was put in place. I was then taken to my room feeling pretty good about myself — I had come through all the procedures successfully.

Unfortunately, it was not going to be as simple as that though. At first, it was not thought that all things went quite a smoothly as we had hoped. I had a few weeks of anxiety, coupled with a few doctor appointments. To make a long story short, I underwent some tests that concluded the operation was a success, and the stint that had been inserted was performing satisfactorily. After all of this information was confirmed, I was given the go ahead to participate in therapy at St. Agnes Hospital. That was a big help to me. The nurses at my workouts were fantastic. I experienced a complete recovery and feel very good.

God willing, I will continue to feel as good now as I have in the past. I want to extend a special thanks to Dr. Telles and his staff for all of their help during my recovery. From September 2005 to now, I have been enjoying life to the fullest. The good Lord willing, I will reach the age of Connie Mack, my old boss.

That's me on the opposite page, arm raised in triumph at our ballpark, with my brother-in-law, Rex Babcock. That park is a great place to watch a game and I enjoy all of the time I spend there.

Triple-A Comes to Fresno

A quest for baseball

I met John Carbray and Diane Engelken, owners of a company named Projects West, in the summer of 1993. Projects West promoted outdoor concerts, most of the time in conjunction with baseball games, drawing bigger crowds with entertainment following the game. The company was very successful.

When I met John that summer, his dream was to build a multi-purpose baseball stadium in Fresno. Not only would this stadium be used for baseball, but for soccer, outdoor concerts, motorcross, and all other types of events. I spent a week or so with John discussing the vision he had. He certainly was not a wealthy man, at least not wealthy enough to build what was then to be a $28,000,000 stadium. To lay the groundwork a proposal had to be made to the city of Fresno — we hoped to receive exclusive rights to pursue his dream. Originally, the stadium was to be 15,000 seats, double-decked with skyboxes. I was 69 years young at the time, semi-retired, and living on my baseball pension and social security. John's income came primarily from Projects West but there was no money to pay salaries. I agreed to come aboard for gas and meal money because I knew I would be traveling around the San Joaquin Valley, gathering investors for the project, and speaking to service clubs and business organizations.

During this time, we printed a paper called the *Stadium Scene* that reported news from the Fresno City Council and the mayor's office. This was the up-to-date baseball news source for all those interested. For Rick Finlay and myself, it was our only source of income related to this endeavor. We delivered these papers to businesses who would then distribute them to the public. My 16 years in radio and television certainly opened many doors. As a former commentator and play-by-play announcer for Fresno State University, I was able to make television and radio appearances, getting the word out to the public. I'd always tell a number of baseball stories and then, of course, talk about the dream of John and Diane. By now it was also a dream of mine as well — I wanted a multi-purpose stadium in downtown Fresno.

Not much happened on the project in 1993. Rick and I were busy getting the *Stadium Scene* out, and I was making about 3 appearances a week with the

That's me in the Grizzlies' sweat shirt with Rick Finlay, a fellow employee of The Diamond Group.

We were working hard on the stadium project right from the start. Here I am with John & Diane Carbray, founders and builders of Grizzlies Stadium.

service clubs telling our story. The progress was very slow to say the least. In the meantime John was like a cat on a hot tin roof. Sometimes, he would join me in my meetings, but usually he had enough on his own agenda to keep him busy. He was in touch with the city on a daily basis and fielded comments that were regularly questioning the stadium project. The mayor, Jim Patterson, was always against the idea. For the most part we seemed to get a pass from the city council. Though, John was referred to in a less than complimentary manner by some. It was embarrassing at times to sit before the city council and hear what they had to say.

In the early going, we were either trying to get our own financing or work with the city to help finance it. In the meantime, Diane was taking care of the office, paying the bills and, I am quite sure, doing a lot of research on other stadium projects. Diane would then give this information to John to use when he appeared before the city council. It was a great experience traveling all through the valley talking with people in different towns. I recall one service club in the southern valley where there was an open bar before dinner. Bill Gorman, our general manager, was along with me. Though we did not drink, you can imagine the problem we faced after a rather long dinner. By the time the program started, many of those in attendance were done. Bill and I laughed our way through the program because most of the guys were asleep in their plates! Needless to say, we sold no box seats or game packages.

From 1993 through 1995, I averaged about 3 appearances per week. Think about this — I was selling season tickets to watch a team we did not own, play in a stadium that was not built — you want to talk strange! The fans of San Joaquin Valley baseball wanted it back, though, and were willing to pitch-in to make it happen. Amazingly, we collected over 3,000 deposits for season tickets.

John and Diane had been partners in business for many years, and in 1995 they decided to get married. Diane made a beautiful bride and John was a fantastic groom. It was a great wedding, followed by a great party. Diane's family from Kansas attended as did John's two sons from a previous marriage, to go along with the many other family and friends.

By 1995, complications were really starting to set in. John Carbray had been negotiating for a Triple-A franchise in the Pacific Coast League. Portland, Tacoma, Tucson and Phoenix all became a part of the picture. Carbray was

That's John Carbray and I with the great Willie Mays. Talk about a guy that could do it all — Mays was one of the best all-around players I ever saw play the game.

always on the telephone with Bill Cutler, president of the PCL. Then something great happened. The city of Phoenix was awarded a major league franchise in expansion, and the Phoenix Triple-A franchise had to be moved. Phoenix had a working agreement with the San Francisco Giants of the National League and the Phoenix owners would not sell. So John bought the Tucson franchise, helped Phoenix move to Tucson and The Diamond Group had its franchise. Unfortunately, there was still no place to play.

Both Phoenix and Tucson were allowed to play their 1997 PCL seasons in their respective cities because the stadium for the Phoenix Diamondbacks would not be ready until the 1998 season. The Diamond Group now had expanded to well over 60 investors. Among those investors, Tim Cullen was key. A former big leaguer, Tim co-owned 2 minor league franchises in the north and east coast regions. Tim contacted his close friend — an old schoolmate and business associate from the bay area. I won't mention all the names, but they represented about $8,000,000. That's how you make these things happen.

Now we own a Triple-A baseball franchise, but the new all-purpose stadium is still just a dream. However, our progress toward that end was being slowed by politics. It was so frustrating at times that we considered moving the franchise to another city. While all this was going on John Carbray had opened negotiations with Fresno State University to use their on-campus baseball field. It is one of the best college baseball diamonds on the west coast. Unfortunately, it did not meet the Triple-A standards. The president of the school and the baseball coach both agreed to let us add bleachers, and build a clubhouse. All of the work was supervised by Glenn Wolf, and how we managed to get all that work done is still a mystery to me. As things stood, it looked like we were ready to bring professional baseball back to Fresno after 11 years of absence.

It was not an easy task to get a college ball park ready for professional baseball. Additional stands were installed, and all new lighting added. A new scoreboard was put in place, additional snack bars were installed and new bathroom facilities were built. Glenn Wolf, who saw that all of these projects were completed properly, was the lead man in this effort. By the way, we had to build a clubhouse as well — no small task. We were now finally ready to open the 1998 Triple-A baseball season. Our affiliation was with the San Francisco Giants of the National League. When baseball left Fresno earlier, the affiliation was with the Giants as well, only it was a Class-A team in the California League.

Before I go any further in regards to bringing baseball back to Fresno, I would like to tell you a little bit more about John and Diane Carbray. John was quite different from anyone that I had ever met before — that's not a bad thing, though. It's difficult to be friends, while being involved in a business venture at the same time. I didn't always know how to separate the two. I consider him to be a fine businessman, and it seemed he could get things done regarding the baseball franchise and the building of a stadium when necessary. John may have never owned a baseball franchise or built a stadium before the Fresno project, though he has had many affiliations with professional sports teams in the past. John is certainly a man of character — his perseverance was amazing during this project. He refused to take no for an answer. He had a dream that he was going to make a reality. Through his many challenges with Fresno City Council members, and their belittling, he never gave up. I believe they were truly jealous. I really believe his intelligence, and drive simply won out over their attempts to block him. That's how we accomplished the building of the multi-purpose stadium in use today, long after most of the city council folks are long gone.

What many people don't know is that Jim Patterson, the mayor of Fresno, was in opposition to the building the stadium. Ironically enough, it was the same Jim Patterson that gave the final go-ahead to the project. The mayor at a public meeting offered to build the stadium as proposed, if John would sign a lease for $1,500,000 a year. Carbray jumped from his chair and accepted — the rest is stadium history.

Let's move forward to my relationship with John as we approach baseball in Fresno. By 1997, many investors had signed on, and The Diamond Group was hiring a sales manager, sales people and ticket managers just to name a few. All of these folks were salaried, and that was good. Unfortunately, when it came to Gus, it seems the door was perpetually closed. I thought I had done a pretty good job for John and The Diamond Group. I wanted to negotiate the salary that I felt I was entitled to receive. In the beginning, when I was told of his dream he said, "When we got everything settled, you will be making a substantial income." That just wasn't happening, and my relationship was beginning to get difficult with both John and Diane. We talked on many occasions, and fortunately a deal was finally worked out. We shook on the deal and that was that. Now, he had a board of directors to deal with in getting 1998 inaugural season underway.

The league we were a member of had 16 teams comprised of four divisions. The Grizzlies played at Bieden Field on the campus of Fresno State University. The first game saw over 6,000 pack the stadium with the usual fly over by the local air base, fire works, flag raising — the whole show. The first skipper for our new Fresno club was a former All-Star third baseman with the San Francisco Giants, Jimmy Davenport. I believe he is the best manager the Grizzlies have had to date. He led us to the division title, although they lost in the playoffs. That evening the ball club rewarded the huge crowd with victory. The event was a big success, and the news really got out about baseball returning to Fresno after 11 years. I should also mention that professional baseball had not left the valley completely. About 40 miles south of Fresno, in Visalia, there is a Class-A team in the California League. That ballclub enjoys great success, with baseball fans traveling from the surrounding areas to see a game.

Though the big crowd certainly gave us all a very optimistic view, the college ballpark was built to only accommodate 2,500 fans — not 6,000! The result of these tremendous crowds was obvious. Concessions were slow and the restrooms were always packed. Nonetheless, fans came and really seemed to enjoy the games. For the time being, everyone involved seemed satisfied. It was fairly easy to be comfortable knowing that down the road, the all-purpose downtown Fresno Stadium would be ready. The average attendance was about 4,000 per game. The stadium had about 3,200 seats in the main grandstand. We added bleacher seats to hold an additional 3,000.

We spent 4 years playing at Bieden Field. After our second year in the league there was a growing concern about the time table for the stadium. At this point, there was little or no headway being made on the new downtown stadium. The Diamond Group even had fears that we may have to move or sell the franchise. I have no idea how many meetings took place with the city and the league during this time. Carbray looked worn out everyday — he appeared to have taken on a herd of elephant's, head-on and lost. To make matters worse, the players that were being sent to Fresno by the Giants were complaining about the field and clubhouse conditions. That used to really get my anger up. I played in worse facilities in the bigs — these kids have no idea what it's like to play in difficult conditions. And take me at my word — I really mean that!

Many of the players we had to deal with were really spoiled rotten. I remember back in the day, I played in a cornfield that had been converted into a baseball diamond. When a ball was hit on the ground to left, you had to field it between the rows. To right, you had to learn to catch it on the proper hop. Oh man, the good ole days in the early '40s. I played in one park that had a light pole about four feet in foul territory, with a big flood light aimed right at the pitcher so you could see him. As a runner on base, you had to make a decision as you rounded third — should I go inside or outside the light pole on my way to the plate. These spoiled, modern players were crying about conditions at Bieden Field — give me a break. There were many ballparks around the league that were not even as good as Bieden Field to begin with. I think you get my drift.

Over those 4 seasons at Bieden Field we did very well. The team played relatively good the first 2 seasons, but was not a real money-maker. A funny story in all of this was the building of the new stadium in Sacramento. Art Savage was a former member of The Diamond Group who was involved in negotiations for the stadium in Fresno in the beginning. After dealing with all of the delay tactics the mayor and city council had to offer, Art took his ideas to Sacramento. There he was able to help build a stadium, 2 years before we would complete ours in Fresno — go figure. Their club had a working agreement with the Oakland Athletics of the American League.

When 2000 rolled around, a new mayor was to be elected, and some changes on the city council seemed imminent. The Diamond Group had a fresh, new attitude about its dream — a downtown multi-purpose stadium. There was a whole new attitude among The Diamond Group people. We began that season believing that we might be in our new facility for the 2001 season — unfortunately, it was not meant to be.

The 2001 season was played at Bieden once again. At this time the Giants were getting the reputation of having one of the worst minor league systems in baseball, and of course the Fresno Grizzlies suffered. We finished last in our division 2 years in a row. In fact, we had the worst record in the PCL during both of those seasons. Though they were difficult seasons, we did get to see some good, young talent come through Fresno. It was really fun to watch the games, and talk with fans about these young players. It was an exiting time for all of us. We would stay after games, and chat with the fans and the local investors about the games and the players. Fans usually stayed until the final out. We enjoyed being part of the new team in town, and many of would hang around and chat.

It was finally scheduled to happen in 2002 — our new stadium was to be ready. Ready on-time was an entirely different issue, though. We had to open on the road, playing in Pac Bell Park in San Francisco. It was not until the first week in May that we played our opening game in the new stadium — it was some kind of night though! It was a sell-out crowd, the Navy jets performed a fly-over and the American flag waving was everywhere. Following the game, John Carbray brought in a spectacular fireworks show. Unfortunately, the season did not go as well as opening night. We finished 30 games under the .500 mark, winding up in last place under manager Len Sakata. Len was a former big league ball player, of Japanese heritage. He did not speak Spanish, and we had about 10 players that spoke only Spanish — this proved to be an issue. No doubt, communication became a major factor on that club. With the arrival of more foreign players each season these days though, it seems the language barrier is solved more easily all of time. That was only one part of problem though — behind the scenes, there were bigger fish to fry.

The front office presented many problems. From my perspective, John and Diane were being undermined on the inside. Seems there was quite an appetite for the chief of the board of directors position. John and Diane were going to be voted out. It's a very long story but Carbray was a lame duck in July of 2002. He completed his term through the last day of December, packed his bags and left, much to the sorrow of many. There were also those that were happy, though I consider most of them to be back stabbers.

The beginning of the 2003 saw Scott Hulme take over as president. Many changes were made. Rick Roush became a power-player and I got the word that he wanted to fire me. A couple of the club's executives, Bill Gorman and Dave Martin, went to bat for me. I didn't even realize this was going on until mid-summer. To me, the reason for all of this was quite simple — this power-player was letting his ego get the best of him. Later that year, Tim Cullen was fired. Tim was the vice president and a big investor in The Diamond Group. When that happened we all knew that no job was safe. I could list many names, but it suffices to say, John Carbray told me this was the board he had put together, and they had turned on him. Roush, now the president of the new board of directors, led a group which knew little or nothing about baseball.

During my 11 years with the club, I viewed myself as a contributing part of the team. I really thought I would always be there. Unfortunately, I forgot the power of the corporate structure — there is no security. I should have known with the departure of John Carbray and his wife, Diane, as well as Tim Cullen's dismissal, that my days were numbered. It was very tough to be told by a general manager of Class-A ball club, that there was no place for me in their organization. I was asked if I wanted to be an independent agent or something along that line — I would no longer be an employee of the Grizzlies. I would be allowed to broadcast a few games with the new general manager's permission. The way it was all handled was an insult to me. General manager Bill Gorman was still there, but he was treated terribly — inhumane if you ask me. I suppose this type of thing actually happens with some regularity. I was never involved with it, though. It was tough for me to get past the entire incident. I could not understand how the group of investors could let the executives running the club almost go into bankruptcy. From all I gather now, it seems their hands were tied. And so were mine to some degree. I was 81 years young when they showed me to the door. Needless-to-say, job opportunities don't come pouring in at my age so I became officially retired — for the time being anyway.

In my tenure with The Diamond Group, I met many new people, and spent a lot of quality time with old friends. Tom Sommers was a jewel of a guy, and one of our leading citizens. He played some professional baseball and spent 10 years in the front office of the California Angels. Dick Ellsworth, top man with one of the largest real estate firms in California and a veteran of big league baseball, had a lot to do with the success of the stadium being built. He was a member of the advisory board in the early going. Dick and I had many chats about the players on the field sent to us by the San Francisco Giants. Jim Maloney, another big leaguer and author of 3 no-hitters, was always talking baseball with the fans and helping to remind people about season tickets. Jim and Dick have a skybox named after them. Joined by Jack Hanna, Stan Oken, Tim Cullen and many others, it was a great pleasure to talk baseball with them. My good friend and golfing partner Hal Britton plays golf every week with me, and during baseball season attend many games. We always had our season tickets too — the club supplied mine until 2004 season.

During my first tour with Fresno, I really had some great highlights. In addition to working with some great people, I got to broadcast a few games with Johnny Doskow in 1998-2000 and Dennis Higgins for 2001-2002. Also joining the team was Jason Anaforian. Since I had worked in broadcasting previously, getting back in the booth was like riding a bike, and I really enjoyed it. My final year was spent with Jason and Doug Greenwald. The broadcasting experience in Fresno was truly a treat for me. I typically did color, but handled the play-by-play duties at times. I especially liked doing color as it gave me the opportunity to tell stories of my playing days.

Though my time had ended with the ball club, it was not that long before I would become a part of Fresno baseball again.

New Life with the Grizzlies
I'm back and better than ever

Chris Cummings and his associates purchased the Fresno Grizzlies baseball team in 2006. At that time, they remained affiliated with the San Francisco Giants of the National League. Pat Fillipone was still the general manager, and the team was set to play in the Pacific Coast League. They finished last for the fifth or sixth time in their 9 years of minor league existence. The ownership group included former big league hurler, Dick Ellsworth.

At the end of the 2006 baseball season, Mr. Fillipone resigned. Brian Glover, a partner in ownership, stepped in as the new general manager. After the season had ended, new ownership announced their plans for the upcoming 2007 season. More emphasis would be placed on entertainment other than baseball, and quite a few dollars were spent on improvements in the stadium. In addition to baseball and high school football games, which were already there, soccer and some outdoor concerts were added to boost the revenue. Grizzlies Stadium also took on the new name of Chukchansi Park. The naming rights for the stadium went for a figure of about $15,000,000 over a 15 year period. A good deal for both parties.

The announcement of the new activities for the stadium by the new

The two pictures above are at the new stadium. Up top is a plaque with a few of my baseball accomplishments and after you're done reading that catch a quick bite to eat at Ozark Ike's Grand Slam.

ownership group was met with great approval by the fans. The new general manager and part-owner, Brian Glover, hired new people to get ready for the 2007 baseball season. The new stadium that was completed in 2002 was now to be a multi-purpose facility that was to house baseball, football, soccer and outdoor concerts.

There was another addition to the Grizzlies family that was going to hit a little closer to home for me, though. The Grizzlies contacted me — excutive Josh Phanco asked me about coming back to join the new administration. I met several times with Josh and other executives Mike Maiorano and Andrew Stuebner, as well as owner, Chris Cummings, and his partner, Brian Glover. I agreed to join the new organization on a part-time basis as the team ambassador. I will be their representative and speak at service clubs and other organizations. It will be a familiar tour of duty for me — one that I have done many times before and enjoyed greatly.

It was made official, and in February of 2007, I'm again a member of the Fresno Grizzlies. It has been an enjoyable return trip for me. My title is "The Ambassador" — it has a really good ring to it. I suppose you could look at it as though I am trying on a new kind of baseball uniform. I have met with several service clubs and attended other outings, and it has really been fun. I have had the opportunity to meet with Chris Cummings several times and found him to be a very enlightening person. Much to my delight, he has expressed an interest in my book and has agreed to help me market it including a signing at the ballpark next year. That sure brought a big smile to this old ballplayer's face!

Cummings is truly interested in the Fresno community and will certainly become more than just a baseball owner — he will be a community leader. He recently purchased the ice hockey franchise as well and has a great interest in building in downtown Fresno. April 5, 2007 was opening night a Chukchansi Park and over 11,500 fans packed the park. The Grizzlies defeated the Portland ballclub 9-4. Yours truly was honored with a great introduction that got the season underway in style. I hope to continue my service to the new organization for many years to come.

On the opposite page is a nice shot of me at the dish at (the then new) Veteran's Stadium in Philly. How do you like the make-shift home plate?

TALKING TO GUS

My Greatest Teammate

You've always got a friend

During my baseball career I played with and against some of the greatest players of all-time. Still, it was several years after I had retired from the game, that I met my greatest teammate of all.

I had settled down nicely into a position in radio and television following baseball. I met some great folks and became golfing buddies with a few that attended Northwest Baptist Church. I started going on Sundays, decided I liked it and joined. Now, I was not unfamiliar with church. My family was a church-going group, and many still are today. I always knew God and many of the *Bible* stories. That said, I more or less lived the first 40 years of my life giving little thought beyond that point. Many of the people I attended church with at that time seemed to have something I didn't — complete peace of mind. A couple years went by and my wife, Marla and I had become regulars at Northwest Baptist Church, but, for me there was still something missing. My friends had something I just couldn't seem to find — it's that total peace of mind.

The church was planning a men's retreat, and my plan was to be a part of it along with my church-going buddies. It was one of the best decisions I would ever make. It was at this retreat that I was asked to join the others in a prayer, accepting Jesus Christ as my Lord and Savior. It was at that moment I met my greatest teammate. I was amazed at just how much he knew about me. In the beginning we didn't talk very much. He didn't say very much to me because I didn't ask him anything. As time passed, we began to have some silent conversations.

I discovered that way back in my childhood he was always near me — I just didn't realize it. I remember a few times during my baseball career that I would walk into a bar with my friends to have a drink. He was spiritually telling me that he knew each and everyone — no secrets here. He even told me about the time when I broke my shoulder in Cleveland. It was an internal compound fracture with the bone almost penetrating my jugular vein. I can remember saying, "God help me!" I asked him, "Why did you let me try to make such a dumb play?" In spirit He answered, "I can't stop you from making dumb plays, but I was there to keep that bone from penetrating your lifeline." I discovered that on the occasions we make dumb moves, He is always there.

To my brothers and sisters in Christ, you know what that journey is like — the last 40-plus years for me. I have watched, along with Marla, so many of my family grow in the Lord. Every chance I get to praise Him in public, I try do so. How could I write a book without finding a place to thank Him for giving me a career and family to write about.

I have given my testimony many times as to how the Lord has come into my life. I have gone to the Lord many times for my own health, as well as others. I have turned over my finances and family affairs to Him. I have never prayed for a base hit, but I have prayed to perform well. He is not concerned with my hitting, He is concerned with my soul. The Lord hears every prayer, but does not answer them all. We sometimes pray foolishly or for things that are not in His plan. For that matter, they may not be in our best interest, only we don't know this — He does. The Lord Jesus said, "He that believes in Me and my Father in Heaven shall have everlasting life." Accept the Lord and follow Him — that is what I believe.

One of the greatest testimonies of my life was in 1992. I was stricken with colon cancer, and it ended up being a double operation. Many of the nurses and doctors didn't think that I would make it — I had so much to live for, though. Marla, never gave up at anytime. She took care of me each and everyday. A lot of tender, loving care sure was the answer. It was only later that I found out on many occasions when I thought she was in the cafeteria having coffee, she was in the chapel praying for my recovery. My good friend and pastor, Bufe Karraker, came to visit me at the hospital, and my condition was not good. We took a few moments for prayer. Later, when the good Lord had brought me back to life, I joked with Bufe telling him that I thought he was giving me my last rites.

All kidding aside, it was a tough recovery that went something like this. The doctors told me I would have to sit up, as I had been down for over 30 days. I sat up on the side of the bed, and everything I saw out the window was blurred. That's anything but a warm, fuzzy feeling inside. Finally, after some time and adjustment, a degree of vision came to me, and I saw the birds flying around outside — I've never been so happy to see a few birds flying around in my life! I prayed to the Lord, who created those birds, asking that if He could find them a place to live, water to drink, and food to eat, could He also return me to my place in life? From that very day forward I began to improve. It took me a total of 4 years to recover completely. Here it is the year 2007, and I am writing of these experiences in my book. Praise the Lord!

The Creator

My thoughts on the good Lord

I just came in from my patio out back where I was meditating for an hour. You may ask, "Meditating about what?" Easy answer — God, the creator. Then you may say, "Who is God?" Well, God created Heaven and Earth. He created the world we live in, but with no guarantees.

One thing written is, "Believe in my son, Jesus Christ, and I will give you everlasting life." When God created the Earth, long before mankind, He also created all the animals that walk the land, all the birds in the sky and all the fish in the water. He made it possible for them all to live in a habitat, complete with food to eat and water to drink. But there were no guarantees.

Let's take, for example, a pair of loving doves. What could be a more appropriate example of peace? Now, I fully realize that when mankind arrived in the form of Adam and Eve, man was given dominion over all of the animals. You may be asking me another question by now, "What is on my mind?" It is this — If a pair of loving doves survive to mate, builds a nest, and the mother lays her eggs, many things can happen. Many of them are bad. While mother dove is sitting on her eggs, a blue jay or a mocking bird, both created by God, destroys her home. I know the answer, but still find it disturbing. If the nest is not sheltered or hidden enough, along comes someone's favorite cat. Odds are the cat will have a meal.

I understand the food chain is a fact of life (and death) for all animals — they survive off the levels below them to stay alive. That's just the way God made it. But it's not a sin to question God. Don't you wonder? Death comes to everyone, but for some it's harder than for others. Don't you wonder why? God placed Adam and Eve in paradise, and soon they were faced with the big test. They failed, and along came Satan. The world has been greatly influenced by him ever since. At one point God was so disappointed in man, that he sought out the most God-fearing man on Earth, Noah, to build his ark. I think you all know that story.

God certainly put a lot of good in man. Unfortunately, for all the good, many men have turned bad and become evil. God spoke often in the old testament about evil men. We have an abundance of that in today's world.

Today, it seems to come from all directions when it involves our country, to be specific. I see evil men trying to destroy the United States from other countries. Then there are evil men in the U.S. doing their best to wreak havoc. Unfortunately, in these times it has become very hard to know who you can trust. When the time of Noah was over, the world of man became evil again. This time, God sent His only begotten son, Jesus Christ, born to the virgin Mary, to save us from our sins, promising us eternal life. Many believe that soon we will see the return of the Savior, who will rule the world and give mankind ever-lasting peace. Many do not believe that this will take place. Don't you wonder about God the Creator?

Gus – The American
A quick political thought

I was born in America.

I grew up as an American.

I went to elementary school as an American.

I went to junior high and high school as an American.

I fought in the U.S. Navy as an American.

I played the American game of baseball.

Then, about 1970, I noticed that things began to change. Groups began to break off from America and develop other philosophies. I thought that this was not a part of the America that I knew and grew up in. At the time, it was said, this was good for America. At this time, 2007, I don't buy it. We are now a country full of separation. When I was a young man growing up in America, the leaders in Washington were not bitter enemies as they have become today — I can remember when we had Democrats and Republicans who could work together for a common cause.

Now these groups I am speaking of have obtained so much political clout that we live in a country divided. Members of one party really hate members of the other. You ask, "How do I know that?" The same way that you know it — they say it on television, over an over again. Perhaps I am a little old fashioned, but this is not America — at least not the one I grew up in. There are over 300 million people that make up America. About half of those believe differently than I do. We are called the United States, but we won't be for much longer at the rate we are being torn apart.

To me, one of the problems is the denotation of red and blue states. It separates us so distinctly, much like we are separated by class envy. I simply don't believe this is a productive way to look at the country. We seem to have so many evil people living here. I say evil people because many, seemingly, hate this country. Still, they live here because we were developed as a nation under God's law, and I hope that won't ever change, though many are trying to change that.

Fortunately, I do not have a fear because as the *Bible* tells me, "Fear and faith do not go together." Certain fear, though, for many these days in our nation, is the fear of Iran or Iraq and other terrorist nations. For me, however, I have a deepening concern about the people of our own country. A look in the mirror at times can be a real awakening in so many ways. I feel we are being misled by some of our own politicians. It seems at times as if some of the liberal leaders are against protecting our country the way I believe we should be protected. The conservatives, as well, have some issues. I believe our nation is more divided now than anytime in history. During my life, I can't remember a time when Christians have been more criticized than these days. We are a country divided and I honestly believe that most folks realize this. There are too many people that have power in Washington that do not believe in God — The Creator. That makes them an enemy of the God-loving American.

I never thought I would live to see the day when our elected officials sent to Washington would lie, cheat, steal and actually hate their fellow man. What influence do you think that has on a real American citizens — it's no wonder we have so much hatred among so many. In addition, the kids of today get off on the wrong track, and the parents are frequently blamed. In some cases I realize that is just, but kids read and watch the media, too. To me, these terrible habits for many kids can start with the hatred spewed by the country's leaders. I hope I live to see the day when our elected officials begin to work for our country and its people instead of perpetuating things for themselves — the greed factor. I believe it all starts with who we call the leaders in our Capitol in Washington, DC — *God Bless America.*

Golf by Numbers
I love this game

I admire talented golfers — the top professionals. Players like Nicklaus, Palmer, Player, Snead and many others from my era. Many other professional athletes from the ranks of baseball, football, basketball and other sports, take up golf, and some even become pretty good. By in large though, most of us simply become hackers, having a great time nonetheless. Ted Williams once said, "Hitting a baseball thrown at better than 95 MPH is the hardest thing to do in sports." I agree with Ted's statement, however, hitting a low draw or a high fade and spin on short shots, as the pros do today, is one tough thing to do. What Williams is saying, though, is almost anyone can tee up a golf ball and hit it. Not many can step into the batter's box and hit a 95 MPH fastball.

Like so many athletes from all sports, I love to play golf. If I break 90 when I go out, I consider it a good day, noting that we really don't track how many times we improve the position of our ball. I have had the pleasure of playing with some of the touring golf professionals. Guys like Bill Glasson, Jerry Heard, Shelly Hamlin — I simply marvel at how adept they are at playing this game. There's no doubt, I am a true fan of golf. When it's sports time on television, I'm more interested in golf than football, baseball or even basketball. Officiating often takes me out of basketball and football — too frustrating at times. I never see an official in golf alter the play, and very few times does an umpire make a poor decision in baseball that actually costs a team the game.

I love to tee it up about 8:00 AM on any course and see if I can par a couple of holes. Every city in the country has a few great golf courses. If folks would turn their cell phones off and take-in the beauty of some of these great courses they would enjoy the game more than ever. Not too many things bother me on the course, but a cell phone does. I know golf pros despise crowd noise, and I can understand why. That said, they should have to tee off with a Philadelphia baseball crowd near by, heckling them for a real-life baseball experience. I do, however, understand the concentration part of the game. My hacker friends and I play for fun. We know how to take care of our playground, too. We fill our divots and fix our ball marks on the greens. We are also proud of our score cards. One will always ask the other, "How many pars did you have?" Followed by, "Lets have a beer and count them." I believe the professional golfers of today are some of our best athletes.

My golf thoughts wouldn't be complete without letting you all in on one story in particular. Well, we had been hit with quite a bit of bad weather on the coast. It seemed many prayers were answered as Jesus and Moses came down to take a look as man did his repair work. While here, Jesus asked Moses, "Would you like to play a round of golf at Pebble Beach?" They agreed that when man got things squared away, they would return to play. Several months later they did so. Jesus got a starting time, and they got under way. When they reached a hole requiring you hit over or around the water, Jesus decided to go over. He put his ball on the tee, and chose his five-iron club. Moses said to Jesus, "You can't reach that green with a five-iron." Jesus replied, "Jack Nicklaus did it — if Jack can do it, I can do it." Jesus hit the five-iron, and it gets about halfway there, and falls into the water. Jesus tells Moses, "Go get that ball please." Moses, shaking his head, parts the water and gets the ball. He returns, and asks Jesus to change clubs, saying, "You can't reach that green with a five-iron." Jesus thought to himself, Nicklaus did it — I can do it. He hits the five-iron again with the same result. Turning to Moses, he asks again for the retrieval of his ball. Moses says, "I'll get it this time, but the next water ball is your problem." Jesus tees it up and swings again with the same result — the water! Shaking his head in disbelief, Jesus starts out walking across the water to get his ball. About this time a foursome approaches from behind, and they're astonished to see Jesus walking across the water. In complete shock, one golfer asks Moses, "Who does that guy think he is — Jesus Christ?" Moses thinks for a moment and replies, "No — Jack Nicklaus." That's your chuckle for the day.

Over the years, I have been involved in many charity golf tournaments. I played in a tournament in Porterville, California, called the KTIP Golf Tournament, and later the Tex and Monte Golf-Arama. Truman Clevenger, a former major league pitcher, runs the show. Clevenger pitched for 7 seasons

As this page shows, reunions are another way through the years we get to see other players, and they're really fun. Here's one that goes back a few days. The 1st row (left to right): Dixie Walker, Roy McMillan, Phil Cavaretta, Harry Walker, Jim Piersall, Monte Irvin, Bobby Richardson, Bill Dickey, Ray Boone and Claude Passeau. The 2nd row (left to right): Roy Campanella, Jim Davenport, Andy Pafko, Stan Hack, Larry French, Cookie Lavagetto, Luke Appling, Allie Reynolds, Yogi Berra, All Zarilla and Jocko Conlan. The 3rd row (left to right): Charlie Grimm, Ernie Banks, Lindsey Nelson, Tom Haller, Mike McCormick, Billy Herman, Dean Chance, Jerry Coleman, Bill Jurges, Joe Cronin, Hank Greenberg, Tom Henrich, Gus Zernial, Eddie Yost and Willie Mays.

I have made mention a few times in this book of the A's Historical Society. The picture here is of one of those reunions that have meant so much to the players who have attended. The 1st row: Randy Gumpert, Sonny Dixon, Irv Hall, Al Brancato, Gus Zernial, George Kell, Joe Ginsberg, Danny Litwhiler, Eddie Joost, Joe Astroth The 2nd row: Carl Scheib, Spook Jacobs, Mickey Vernon, Allie Clark, Joe DeMaestri, Bill Hockenbury, Doug Clemens, Skeeter Kell, Don Hasenmayer, Barney Schultz, Leroy Wheat and John Addison.

in the bigs. Monte Moore was a big league broadcaster for the Oakland Athletics for 20 years — these two gentlemen ran this tournament for 25 years, and gave the proceeds to many schools' athletic programs. More than $800,000 was raised during that time. This tournament had some pretty good athletes participate, too. I can remember Hank Sauer, Jimmy Davenport, Vida Blue, John "Blue Moon" Odom, Lon Simmons, Joe DeMaestri, Ted Bowsfield, Mark Gardner, Bobby Jones, Bob Bennett (a fine baseball coach) and umpires Doug Harvey and Terry Cooney. All these folks were very giving of their time, thus benefiting others in many ways — my hat's off to them.

Many of my baseball friends played quite a bit of golf and were pretty good, too. Hank Sauer was a top amateur golfer that I played with often. He was a very low handicap player. Vic Lombardi, a former major league pitcher, became a teaching-pro and was a one-handicap player. When Vic got into a money game, I could always tell he was going to win at the first tee. He would typically try to talk the group he was playing with into giving him at least two strokes. You golfers know what I am talking about. I would guess Vic won about 75% of the time. Other guys that come to memory who dabbled in the game include Gene Mauch, Gerry Priddy and Peanuts Lowrey. Oh — and then there's Al "Zeke" Zarilla, who I will always remember for his game of golf. I don't think Zeke ever broke a 110!

Golf is a favorite past time of mine, and my favorite course is Sherwood Forest. It is privately owned by the Hanson family. Carol Hanson founded the course. Though I won't go into the entire history, I do want to say that the family has always been great to me — I'll never forget that.

My golfing buddies to this day are Hal Britton and Cliff Mergerdigian. I will be 84 in the summer of 2007, and I'm still determined to play a round or two. I will sure be happy if I can shoot in the '80s. If I am lucky maybe I can find two of my other old golfing buddies, Dick Best and Don Killian. We haven't played much lately, but it would sure be a great time to catch up on everything and enjoy a favorite game of ours.

That's me on the opposite page with my good friend and business partner John Carbray — one of the good guys.

These are just some thoughts from a couple of people I have both respected and admired for many years. I thought I would share them with you in this section of the book.

Play by Play
Announcer Merle Harmon

The year was 1955, but it seems like only yesterday that I reported to my first spring training in West Palm Beach, Florida, as a young play-by-play announcer for the Kansas City Athletics. The team had just moved there from Philadelphia to become the western outpost for Major League Baseball. What a thrill it was to step out on the field of the little stadium named after Connie Mack, the grand old man of baseball, who had owned the team from its inception until forced to sell due to long time financial difficulties.

During the workout that first day of spring training, I met most of the players and they were cordial, but one man greeted me with a big smile and a big handshake. It was Gus Zernial, the guy they called "Ozark Ike," after the famous comic book character. He was the biggest name on the A's roster. He didn't know me from Adam, but I sure knew who he was. At a strapping 6'-4", 215 pounds, he led the American League in home runs and RBIs in 1951.

Gus and I became very good friends. We would take in an occasional movie together when the team was on the road. Our families enjoyed picnics together. My 8-year old son worshipped him. Gus never met a fan he didn't like. He was the most popular player in Kansas City. His legion of loyal fans were shocked when he was traded to Detroit. He was greeted with roaring applause the first time he stepped to the plate at Kansas City Municipal Stadium in a Tiger uniform.

When Gus was considering retirement, he started talking to me about getting into broadcasting. I asked him where he started baseball. He told me it was in a Class-D league in Georgia. I told him he should go to a minor league team and start at the bottom in broadcasting. Learn the business and get the bugs out, then move up the ladder.

A few years later I was driving from Oakland to the San Francisco

Airport, via the San Mateo Bridge, listening to a Fresno State football game. The play-by-play man was doing great job. I thought he was very smooth and professional. But I wondered who he was? I was about half way across the bridge when the radio station came back from a commercial and the announcer identified himself — "This is Gus Zernial," he said. My gosh, I almost crashed my car. I was never more proud of discovering a new colleague with tremendous broadcasting talent, who was an old friend.

Gus and I hooked up later when I was on the coast to broadcast games in Oakland and Anaheim. By then I had learned that in addition to football, he was broadcasting baseball, basketball as well as many other sporting events. He also had a daily show — heck, he owned the market! Gus had paid the price for success in broadcasting just as in baseball — with hard work. Everything he achieved in baseball and broadcasting he earned with good old hard work.

In retirement, Gus is still working hard with a new team. This time he's with the Lord's team, sharing his testimony through conversation, and bringing the Good News to so many. When the time comes, and Gus gets the call to join the Lord's baseball roster in Heaven, that club will be getting a bona-fide home run hitter!

The Triple-A Connection
Team owner John Carbray

I arrived in Fresno in 1991 with the plan of bringing Triple-A baseball and building a modern multi-purpose stadium in Fresno. At first I had quiet meetings with local baseball and political leaders trying to research the viability of, what some thought was, a crazy idea.

Later the next year a somewhat intimidating character named Zernial walked into our office and asked the receptionist, "which office is mine?" She brought me the message and I went out to meet Gus Zernial and my friendship with this big-hearted man was born.

Gus is both well-known and respected throughout the Fresno area and "The Valley" as we call it. His energy, booming voice and infectious enthusiasm for sports and baseball was an encouraging gift to me from heaven.

As a young boy growing up in Los Angeles I was the consummate Los Angeles Angels fan. So of course I knew that Gus played for the hated cross-town Hollywood Stars. At only 12 years old I just knew we were the real "working class" fans who cheered on the Angels. We took the street cars or hitch-hiked to Wrigley Field. The team was owned by Chicago magnate Phil Wrigley and the stadium was a replica of the Cubs home in Chicago. Meanwhile the Stars drew the Hollywood celebrities and my buddies and I thought their fans were the "going just to be seen" type at their games at Gilmore Field. Even now, I still tease him about the short pants the Hollywood Stars wore one season just to get his goat and rile him up.

When Gus joined our staff he energized us both inside and outside the office. Because of his popularity and being well-known as a broadcaster and baseball legend, people took note of his endorsement of the implausible idea that a Triple-A baseball team could play in a new stadium to be built in Fresno. It seemed an impossible dream until people started to believe.

I was new to Fresno, but, with an introduction and escort from big Gus, I was welcomed to many a small and medium city here in the Valley, speaking at too many service club lunches and dinners to count. We would "tag-team" our presentation with Gus teeing it up with his days in professional baseball, meeting Marilyn Monroe, stories of the Philadelphia A's and so on. Then I would be the "pitch-man" explaining the idea of a new stadium for all the Valley. He just plain helped give us credibility.

Our group was the "Fresno Diamond Group" and we had to persevere through 9 years of meetings, 3 mayors and finally a financial deal that worked. At one of our countless Fresno City Council meetings, even before he joined our staff, Gus went into action. He gripped the podium in front of the dais to make the point during a heated discussion on why a stadium should be considered and in his booming voice told them, "I'd rather see teenagers carrying a baseball bat than a gun!" The on-looking supporters clapped wildly in the audience and it helped light the fire to join the effort.

Without Gus and his larger-than-life presence, the new downtown Grizzlies Stadium would not exist and Fresno would be without the Triple-A level baseball it deserves.

I love Gus, congratulate and wish him the best with this book, and hope all of you enjoy it.

CLOSE IT OUT
& FAMILY PHOTOS

Up top, that's Marla's sister, Sandy Babcock, with Marla and yours truly.

To the right, I'm sharing a smile with my daughter, Dr. Susan (as I refer to her.)

And to the lower right, my youngest daughter, Lisa, and I are smiling for the camera.

On the previous page we took a moment for a group shot. From left to right are Barry Pearlstein, Ryan, Lisa, Gus, Marla, Addison and Afton holding Jaedyn.

My Family and This Book

A helping hand

This book was written with a great deal of input from my family. This project has certainly been a team effort that has included my wife, Marla Jean, son, James, and daughters, Susan Carol and Lisa Marlane. I married Marla soon after I retired from baseball, and she has been such an important part of my life — the many golf tournaments, speaking engagements, and baseball banquets have always found her to be an enthusiastic participant. She has been a partner in my career as I continued in my second profession. She has heard all the stories I tell over and over, and has met many of my baseball teammates, friends and fans. She has helped me with this book, as well as my life.

Susan lives in Silver Springs, Nevada, and often visits us. When I left the game in 1959, she was only 11-years old. Nonetheless, she remembers many games of the 1950's, as she attended quite a few. Later on she joined me at some of the old-timer games. She entertained the idea of writing a book about dear old Dad, but her profession keeps her very busy. Being a college graduate with numerous degrees, I address her as Dr. Susan. The good doctor helped me with my periods and commas in the book, as well some history. She reminded me in many chapters about my first family and life at that time — this was a huge help to me.

My son, James has added so much to this book during our many conversations about baseball, football and basketball. He freely expresses his feelings about players and the coaching. While I do not always agree with him, I respect his opinions and have used some of his information in my book. His athletic background was diverse playing football, basketball and baseball in high school. He is an avid sports fan and has been very interested in how I am putting this book together.

Lisa missed my playing days of baseball, but she was around for my radio and television career. Although it didn't take long for her to know her father was a former major league ball player, she knew me best as a television and radio broadcaster. My work in television and radio often kept me away from home. This kept me from developing that close bond all parents want to have with their children. This was an unfortunate pitfall of my second career.

Lisa worked several jobs after graduating from high school, married and now has 4 children Afton, Adam, Adison and Ryan. Barry Pearlstein, her husband, is a great father and very good son-in-law.

Lisa's input to this book is built around my television and radio work. She makes no bones about the fact that I was absent from home life quite a bit. However, she is proud of her Dad. I am happy to be good friends with both of my daughters. Afton, Lisa's first daughter, gave birth to a young lady by the name of Jaedyn, our first great grandchild. That really created new life for Marla and I — truly amazing!

My children come to see me regularly, and that is what it is all about. I am a very proud husband, father, grandfather and great grandfather — in short, a very lucky man.

A Closing Thought

I hope you enjoyed reading this book, as much as I enjoyed writing it. It really taxed my memory at times, and in doing my research I discovered things about my family, as well as my baseball experiences, that had been hidden away for many seasons. Thinking about the friends, fans, teammates and the many radio and television personalities I've crossed paths with over the years has been refreshing.

What a pleasure it was to have the youngsters in the cities where you play gather for an autograph, or just to say hello. Most, I would never see again — though I must say, you were and still are a big part of my life. Baseball opened so many doors for me. It was my baseball connections that led me to my second careeer in radio and television. They also led me to Bill Bozman and Ronnie Joyner, who helped me put this book together.

I want to give a special thank you to my many friends of the San Joaquin Valley and Fresno areas — you have added much joy to my life. On the golf course, at a luncheon or just walking the neighborhood, I could not have hoped for more. I also want to give thanks to God who provided me with so much of the inspiration for my writing.

Most of all, thanks to my wife, Marla, and our entire family, for helping me do something that I had only dreamed of.

Up top, that's me with my son, Jim.

This is Jim with his son, our grandson, Eziekiel.

Marla and I are enjoying a leisurely evening out.

Above are my grandson, Adam, and his mom, Lisa, at one of his college games. To the left, Adam accepts a few high-fives after hitting a home run.

On the event circuit Marla has always been a trooper — I could not have hoped for better support than she's always given. Here we are pictured again at baseball gathering.

You guessed it — another fabulous evening with my wife. Life is good!

Ryan, the son of Barry and Lisa, proudly displays his catch of the day.

Early Life

Imagine living in the foothills of California

Living a life of calm and serene
Overlooking the field and streams
Values of life you can remember
Enjoying the beautiful fall of September

You know you will never forget
Overlooking all the times that we all regret
Until we have peace of mind and life is set

To my family, friends, baseball fans, writers and sportscasters,
I send this poem to you.

Take the first letter of each line and read from top to bottom.
My feelings to ALL.

STATS & HOMERS

Gus Zernial Career Statistics

Year	Tm	G	AB	R	H	2B	3B	HR	RBI	BB	SO	BA	OBP
1949	CHW	73	198	29	63	17	2	5	38	15	26	.318	.366
1950	CHW	143	543	75	152	16	4	29	93	38	110	.280	.330
1951	TOT	143	571	92	153	30	5	33	129	63	101	.268	.345
	CHW	4	19	2	2	0	0	0	4	2	2	.105	.190
	PHA	139	552	90	151	30	5	33	125	61	99	.274	.350
1952	PHA	145	549	76	144	15	1	29	100	70	87	.262	.347
1953	PHA	147	556	85	158	21	3	42	108	57	79	.284	.355
1954	PHA	97	336	42	84	8	2	14	62	30	60	.250	.316
1955	KCA	120	413	62	105	9	3	30	84	30	90	.254	.304
1956	KCA	109	272	36	61	12	0	16	44	33	66	.224	.315
1957	KCA	131	437	56	103	20	1	27	69	34	84	.236	.290
1958	DET	66	124	8	40	7	1	5	23	6	25	.323	.351
1959	DET	60	132	11	30	4	0	7	26	7	27	.227	.262
11 Seasons		1234	4131	572	1093	159	22	237	776	383	755	.265	.329

Gus Zernial Home Run Record

No.	Date	Team	Pos.	Pitcher	Opp.	Site	Inn.	On
1	04/22/49	CHA	LF	Red Embree	SLA	CHA	4	0
2	05/03/49	CHA	LF	Ray Scarborough	WAS	CHA	2	0
3	05/18/49	CHA	LF	Ellis Kinder	BOS	BOS	5	2
4	09/04/49	CHA	LF	Hal Newhouser	DET	DET	5	0
5	09/21/49	CHA	PH	Joe Page	NYA	NYA	9	2
6	05/06/50	CHA	LF	Chuck Stobbs	BOS	BOS	2	0
7	05/16/50	CHA	LF	Joe Haynes	WAS	CHA	4	2
8	05/22/50	CHA	LF	Al Papai	BOS	CHA	7	1
9	05/28/50	CHA	LF	Early Wynn	CLE	CHA	3	1
				All runs in game from this HR				
10	05/30/50	CHA	LF	Ned Garver	SLA	SLA	3	1
11	05/30/50	CHA	LF	Cliff Fannin	SLA	SLA	5	0
12	06/06/50	CHA	LF	Mel Parnell	BOS	BOS	4	0
13	06/06/50	CHA	LF	Mel Parnell	BOS	BOS	6	0
14	06/13/50	CHA	LF	Tommy Byrne	NYA	CHA	1	1
15	06/25/50	CHA	LF	Lou Brissie	PHA	CHA	5	2
16	06/26/50	CHA	LF	Hal White	DET	DET	1	1
17	06/30/50	CHA	LF	Ned Garver	SLA	CHA	13	0
18	07/02/50	CHA	LF	Fritz Dorish	SLA	CHA	3	2
19	07/08/50	CHA	LF	Duane Pillette	SLA	SLA	6	0
20	07/25/50	CHA	LF	Joe Haynes	WAS	CHA	3	0
21	07/30/50	CHA	LF	Vic Raschi	NYA	CHA	4	0
22	07/30/50	CHA	LF	Vic Raschi	NYA	CHA	8	0
23	07/30/50	CHA	LF	Whitey Ford	NYA	CHA	1	1
24	08/04/50	CHA	LF	Willard Nixon	BOS	CHA	7	1
25	08/20/50	CHA	LF	Mike Garcia	CLE	CLE	7	0
26	08/28/50	CHA	LF	Joe Ostrowski	NYA	NYA	5	1
27	08/31/50	CHA	LF	Walt Masterson	BOS	BOS	8	0
28	09/06/50	CHA	LF	Cliff Fannin	SLA	CHA	6	0
29	09/17/50	CHA	LF	Bob Kuzava	WAS	CHA	4	1
30	09/30/50	CHA	LF	Al Widmar	SLA	CHA	6	1
31	10/01/50	CHA	LF	Ned Garver	SLA	CHA	5	1
32	10/01/50	CHA	LF	Stubby Overmire	SLA	CHA	2	0
33	10/01/50	CHA	LF	Stubby Overmire	SLA	CHA	3	1
34	10/01/50	CHA	LF	Jack Bruner	SLA	CHA	8	1
35	05/13/51	PHA	LF	Spec Shea	NYA	PHA	1	1
36	05/13/51	PHA	LF	Fred Sanford	NYA	PHA	5	0
37	05/15/51	PHA	LF	Dick Starr	SLA	PHA	1	1
				Inside-the-Park HR				
38	05/15/51	PHA	LF	Ned Garver	SLA	PHA	9	0
39	05/16/51	PHA	LF	Cliff Fannin	SLA	PHA	2	1
40	05/16/51	PHA	LF	Duane Pillette	SLA	PHA	5	1
41	05/17/51	PHA	LF	Don Johnson	SLA	PHA	1	1
42	06/02/51	PHA	LF	Joe Dobson	CHA	CHA	5	0
43	06/10/51	PHA	LF	Hal Newhouser	DET	DET	3	1
44	06/15/51	PHA	LF	Ken Holcombe	CHA	PHA	1	3
45	06/19/51	PHA	LF	Hal White	DET	PHA	8	1
46	06/22/51	PHA	LF	Al Widmar	SLA	PHA	4	0
47	06/22/51	PHA	LF	Al Widmar	SLA	PHA	8	0

★ OZARK IKE ★

No.	Date	Team	Pos.	Pitcher	Opp.	Site	Inn.	On
48	06/24/51	PHA	LF	Dick Starr	SLA	PHA	1	1
49	06/24/51	PHA	LF	Dick Starr	SLA	PHA	5	2
50	06/27/51	PHA	LF	Willard Nixon	BOS	BOS	6	1
51	06/29/51	PHA	LF	Joe Haynes	WAS	PHA	3	0
52	07/01/51	PHA	LF	Tom Ferrick	WAS	PHA	7	1
53	07/02/51	PHA	LF	Allie Reynolds	NYA	PHA	9	1
54	07/07/51	PHA	LF	Julio Moreno	WAS	WAS	4	0
55	07/07/51	PHA	LF	Julio Moreno	WAS	WAS	6	1
56	07/12/51	PHA	LF	Dick Starr	SLA	SLA	8	3
57	07/18/51	PHA	LF	Dizzy Trout	DET	DET	8	2
58	08/02/51	PHA	LF	Randy Gumpert	CHA	PHA	5	0
59	08/16/51	PHA	LF	Willard Nixon	BOS	PHA	8	1
60	08/22/51	PHA	LF	Billy Pierce	CHA	CHA	1	1
61	08/22/51	PHA	LF	Joe Dobson	CHA	CHA	1	2
62	08/24/51	PHA	LF	Ned Garver	SLA	SLA	1	2
63	08/2951	PHA	LF	Mike Garcia	CLE	CLE	4	1
64	09/09/51	PHA	LF	Chuck Stobbs	BOS	PHA	6	1
65	09/15/51	PHA	LF	Randy Gumpert	CHA	PHA	6	2
66	09/16/51	PHA	LF	Duke Markell	SLA	PHA	3	1
67	09/26/51	PHA	LF	Bob Kuzava	NYA	NYA	3	1
68	05/08/52	PHA	LF	Lou Sleater	SLA	PHA	1	1
69	05/09/52	PHA	LF	Bob Porterfield	WAS	PHA	5	1
70	05/10/52	PHA	LF	Spec Shea	WAS	PHA	2	0
71	05/18/52	PHA	LF	Bob Feller	CLE	CLE	6	0
72	05/25/52	PHA	LF	Julio Moreno	WAS	WAS	6	0
73	05/27/52	PHA	LF	Ray Scarborough	BOS	BOS	3	1
74	06/02/52	PHA	LF	Ned Garver	SLA	PHA	4	0
75	06/22/52	PHA	LF	Marlin Stuart	DET	DET	1	1
76	06/22/52	PHA	LF	Art Houtteman	DET	DET	3	0
77	06/22/52	PHA	LF	Dick Littlefield	DET	DET	9	1
78	06/28/52	PHA	LF	Johnny Sain	NYA	NYA	1	1
79	06/28/52	PHA	LF	Johnny Sain	NYA	NYA	2	2
80	07/01/52	PHA	LF	Julio Moreno	WAS	PHA	1	1
81	07/04/52	PHA	LF	Mel Parnell	BOS	PHA	6	0
82	07/13/52	PHA	LF	Lou Kretlow	CHA	PHA	4	1
83	07/13/52	PHA	LF	Bill Kennedy	CHA	PHA	7	3
84	08/01/52	PHA	LF	Mike Garcia	CLE	CLE	9	3
85	08/02/52	PHA	LF	Early Wynn	CLE	CLE	8	0
86	08/03/52	PHA	LF	Sam Jones	CLE	CLE	7	1
87	08/07/52	PHA	LF	Dizzy Trout	BOS	PHA	3	2
88	08/07/52	PHA	LF	Mickey McDermott	BOS	PHA	7	0
89	08/16/52	PHA	LF	Walt Masterson	WAS	PHA	6	1
90	08/22/52	PHA	LF	Satchel Paige	SLA	PHA	1	3
91	08/23/52	PHA	LF	Marlin Stuart	SLA	PHA	2	0
92	08/27/52	PHA	LF	Mike Garcia	CLE	PHA	4	0
93	08/29/52	PHA	LF	Ike Delock	BOS	PHA	3	0
94	08/31/52	PHA	LF	Willard Nixon	BOS	PHA	2	0
95	09/23/52	PHA	LF	Walt Masterson	WAS	PHA	1	2
96	09/26/52	PHA	LF	Eddie Lopat	NYA	PHA	6	1
97	04/16/53	PHA	LF	Mel Parnell	BOS	PHA	4	0
98	04/19/53	PHA	LF	Jim McDonald	NYA	PHA	4	0

No.	Date	Team	Pos.	Pitcher	Opp.	Site	Inn.	On
99	04/23/53	PHA	LF	Walt Masterson	WAS	WAS	5	0
100	05/01/53	PHA	LF	Ned Garver	DET	DET	2	0
101	05/16/53	PHA	LF	Hal Erickson	DET	PHA	6	1
102	05/24/53	PHA	LF	Connie Marrero	WAS	WAS	8	0
103	05/27/53	PHA	LF	Marv Grissom	BOS	PHA	8	0
104	05/29/53	PHA	LF	Vic Raschi	NYA	PHA	1	2
105	06/02/53	PHA	LF	Ned Garver	DET	DET	2	0
106	06/03/53	PHA	LF	Dave Madison	DET	DET	7	2
107	06/03/53	PHA	LF	Hal Erickson	DET	DET	9	0
108	06/04/53	PHA	LF	Billy Hoeft	DET	DET	8	0
109	06/07/53	PHA	LF	Bob Feller	CLE	CLE	4	0
110	06/11/53	PHA	LF	Joe Dobson	CHA	CHA	4	1
111	06/11/53	PHA	LF	Bob Keegan	CHA	CHA	7	1
112	06/13/53	PHA	LF	Dick Littlefield	SLA	SLA	5	2
113	06/20/53	PHA	LF	Billy Pierce	CHA	PHA	2	0
114	06/21/53	PHA	LF	Joe Dobson	CHA	PHA	7	0
115	07/06/53	PHA	LF	Johnny Sain	NYA	PHA	8	0
116	07/07/53	PHA	LF	Whitey Ford	NYA	PHA	1	2
117	07/16/53	PHA	LF	Mike Garcia	CLE	CLE	6	0
118	07/25/53	PHA	LF	Mike Fornieles	CHA	CHA	8	0
119	07/30/53	PHA	LF	Mike Blyzka	SLA	PHA	2	0
120	08/01/53	PHA	LF	Bob Feller	CLE	PHA	9	1
121	08/02/53	PHA	LF	Bob Lemon	CLE	PHA	7	0
122	08/05/53	PHA	LF	Joe Dobson	CHA	PHA	2	0
123	08/07/53	PHA	LF	Ralph Branca	DET	PHA	4	0
124	08/09/53	PHA	LF	Dick Marlowe	DET	PHA	1	1
125	08/09/53	PHA	PH	Ray Herbert	DET	PHA	6	3
126	08/19/53	PHA	LF	Ben Flowers	BOS	BOS	4	1
127	08/19/53	PHA	LF	Ben Flowers	BOS	BOS	6	0
128	08/25/53	PHA	LF	Billy Pierce	CHA	CHA	4	0
129	08/25/53	PHA	LF	Billy Pierce	CHA	CHA	8	1
130	08/27/53	PHA	LF	Bob Turley	SLA	SLA	4	0
131	08/28/53	PHA	LF	Duane Pillette	SLA	SLA	1	1
132	09/01/53	PHA	LF	Ned Garver	DET	DET	1	1
133	09/01/53	PHA	LF	Ned Garver	DET	DET	5	0
134	09/07/53	PHA	LF	Bob Porterfield	WAS	PHA	2	0
135	09/19/53	PHA	LF	Spec Shea	WAS	PHA	1	2
136	09/20/53	PHA	LF	Johnny Schmitz	WAS	PHA	2	0
137	09/20/53	PHA	LF	Walt Masterson	WAS	PHA	6	2
				Inside-the-Park HR				
138	09/22/53	PHA	LF	Bob Kuzava	NYA	NYA	8	0
139	04/13/54	PHA	LF	Mel Parnell	BOS	PHA	5	1
140	04/18/54	PHA	LF	Sid Hudson	BOS	BOS	2	0
141	04/18/54	PHA	LF	Sid Hudson	BOS	BOS	4	0
142	05/15/54	PHA	LF	Fritz Dorish	CHA	CHA	6	0
143	05/22/54	PHA	LF	Spec Shea	WAS	WAS	1	2
144	05/26/54	PHA	LF	Leo Kiely	BOS	PHA	3	3
145	05/28/54	PHA	LF	Dean Stone	WAS	PHA	2	0
146	05/28/54	PHA	LF	Dean Stone	WAS	PHA	8	2
147	05/30/54	PHA	LF	Bob Porterfield	WAS	PHA	6	0
148	06/01/54	PHA	LF	Tex Clevenger	BOS	BOS	1	2

No.	Date	Team	Pos.	Pitcher	Opp.	Site	Inn.	On
149	06/01/54	PHA	LF	Bill Werle	BOS	BOS	9	0
150	06/17/54	PHA	PH	Jack Harshman	CHA	CHA	7	2
151	06/27/54	PHA	LF	Joe Coleman	BAL	BAL	4	1
152	07/03/54	PHA	LF	Russ Kemmerer	BOS	BOS	3	1
153	04/18/55	KC	LF	Ray Narleski	CLE	KC?	3	0
154	04/19/55	KC	LF	Herb Score	CLE	KC	4	0
155	04/22/55	KC	LF	Virgil Trucks	CHA	KC	6	0
156	04/27/55	KC	LF	Frank Sullivan	BOS	KC	3	2
157	05/02/55	KC	LF	Johnny Schmitz	WAS	KC	8	0
158	05/04/55	KC	LF	Jim McDonald	BAL	KC	5	0
159	05/08/55	KC	LF	Art Houtteman	CLE	CLE	5	0
160	05/08/55	KC	LF	Mike Garcia	CLE	CLE	4	0
161	05/12/55	KC	LF	Ike Delock	BOS	BOS	3	1
162	05/12/55	KC	LF	Ike Delock	BOS	BOS	5	1
163	05/24/55	KC	PH	George Zuverink	DET	KC	6	2
164	05/29/55	KC	LF	Herb Score	CLE	KC	8	0
165	06/01/55	KC	LF	Johnny Kucks	NYA	KC	7	0
166	06/07/55	KC	LF	Mickey McDermott	WAS	KC	3	0
167	06/15/55	KC	LF	Mel Parnell	BOS	BOS	1	0
168	06/26/55	KC	LF	Don Johnson	BAL	BAL	1	0
169	06/29/55	KC	LF	Bob Feller	CLE	CLE	5	1
170	07/15/55	KC	LF	Jim McDonald	BAL	KC	3	1
171	07/24/55	KC	LF	Whitey Ford	NYA	KC	3	0
172	07/27/55	KC	LF	Dean Stone	WAS	WAS	6	2
173	07/31/55	KC	LF	Bob Wiesler	NYA	NYA	8	1
174	08/05/55	KC	LF	Frank Sullivan	BOS	BOS	3	0
175	08/05/55	KC	LF	Frank Sullivan	BOS	BOS	5	1
176	08/12/55	KC	LF	Art Houtteman	CLE	KC	4	0
177	09/10/55	KC	LF	Webbo Clarke	WAS	WAS	6	0
178	09/10/55	KC	LF	Pedro Ramos	WAS	WAS	9	2
179	09/14/55	KC	LF	Ike Delock	BOS	BOS	7	1
180	09/14/55	KC	LF	George Susce	BOS	BOS	8	3
181	09/18/55	KC	LF	Dick Donovan	CHA	KC	3	3
182	09/24/55	KC	LF	Sandy Consuegra	CHA	CHA	7	1
183	04/20/56	KC	LF	Dick Donovan	CHA	KC	8	0
184	05/06/56	KC	LF	Bob Wiesler	WAS	WAS	5	1
185	05/06/56	KC	LF	Bob Wiesler	WAS	WAS	7	0
186	05/08/56	KC	LF	Hal Brown	BAL	BAL	4	0
187	05/12/56	KC	LF	Early Wynn	CLE	CLE	6	1
188	05/21/56	KC	LF	Tom Sturdivant	NYA	KC	3	0
189	05/26/56	KC	LF	Billy Hoeft	DET	DET	8	1
190	05/28/56	KC	LF	Dixie Howell	CHA	KC	8	1
191	06/13/56	KC	LF	Connie Grob	WAS	WAS	8	0
192	06/21/56	KC	LF	Pedro Ramos	WAS	KC	7	1
193	07/07/56	KC	LF	Herb Score	CLE	KC	1	0
194	07/08/56	KC	LF	Bob Lemon	CLE	KC	8	0
195	08/09/56	KC	LF	Virgil Trucks	DET	DET	1	2
196	08/26/56	KC	LF	Frank Sullivan	BOS	BOS	8	0
197	08/26/56	KC	LF	George Susce	BOS	BOS	9	1
198	09/28/56	KC	PH	Billy Pierce	CHA	KC	7	1
199	04/16/57	KC	LF	Frank Lary	DET	KC	6	0

No.	Date	Team	Pos.	Pitcher	Opp.	Site	Inn.	On
200	04/25/57	KC	LF	Early Wynn	CLE	KC	8	1
201	04/28/57	KC	LF	Jim Wilson	CHA	KC	4	0
202	05/01/57	KC	LF	Dave Sisler	BOS	KC	1	1
203	05/12/57	KC	LF	Early Wynn	CLE	CLE	4	0
204	05/18/57	KC	LF	Bob Chakales	BOS	BOS	5	2
205	05/22/57	KC	LF	Ted Abernathy	WAS	WAS	1	1
206	05/22/57	KC	LF	Tex Clevenger	WAS	WAS	7	0
207	05/26/57	KC	LF	Duke Maas	DET	KC	6	0
208	05/30/57	KC	LF	Duke Maas	DET	DET	5	1
209	06/05/57	KC	LF	Ray Moore	BAL	KC	1	0
210	06/09/57	KC	LF	Frank Sullivan	BOS	KC	3	0
211	06/12/57	KC	LF	Camilo Pascual	WAS	KC	6	1
212	06/21/57	KC	LF	Rudy Minarcin	BOS	BOS	7	0
213	06/23/57	KC	LF	Tom Brewer	BOS	BOS	7	0
214	07/05/57	KC	LF	Jim Bunning	DET	DET	4	0
215	07/20/57	KC	PH	George Zuverink	BAL	KC	9	2
216	08/08/57	KC	LF	Billy Pierce	CHA	CHA	3	2
217	08/11/57	KC	LF	Don Mossi	CLE	CLE	1	1
218	08/11/57	KC	LF	Don Mossi	CLE	CLE	3	0
219	09/13/57	KC	LF	Russ Kemmerer	WAS	WAS	4	1
220	09/14/57	KC	LF	Ralph Lumenti	WAS	WAS	6	0
221	09/17/57	KC	LF	Mike Fornieles	BOS	BOS	1	1
222	09/21/57	KC	LF	Jim Bunning	DET	KC	3	0
223	09/21/57	KC	LF	Chuck Daniel	DET	KC	5	1
224	09/23/57	KC	LF	Don Rudolph	CHA	KC	5	0
225	09/28/57	KC	LF	Paul Foytack	DET	DET	13	1
226	05/04/58	DET	PH	George Zuverink	BAL	BAL	9	0
227	05/22/58	DET	PH	Ryne Duren	NYA	DET	8	0
228	06/06/58	DET	LF	Hal Griggs	WAS	WAS	3	1
229	06/08/58	DET	PH	Pedro Ramos	WAS	WAS	7	0
230	07/22/58	DET	LF	Bob Turley	NYA	DET	9	0
231	06/26/59	DET	PH	Billy O'Dell	BAL	DET	7	0
232	06/27/59	DET	1B	Billy Hoeft	BAL	DET	2	1
233	06/27/59	DET	1B	Arnie Portocarrero	BAL	DET	6	2
234	07/03/59	DET	1B	Early Wynn	CHA	DET	6	2
235	07/11/59	DET	1B	Mudcat Grant	CLE	CLE	4	0
236	08/07/59	DET	1B	Bill Monbouquette	BOS	BOS	4	0
237	08/15/59	DET	1B	Herb Score	CLE	DET	3	0

List compiled by: David Vincent, author of "Home Run: The Definitive History of Baseball's Ultimate Weapon"

GENERAL INDEX

(bold page numbers indicate person in photograph)

Index compiled by: Sumner Hunnewell